HELL NO

Also by Tom Hayden

The Other Side (with Staughton Lynd) (1966)
Rebellion in Newark: Official Violence and Ghetto Response (1967)
*Rebellion and Repression: Testimony by Tom Hayden Before the National
    Commission on the Causes and Prevention of Violence, and the House
    Un-American Activities Committee* (1969)
Trial (1970)
The Love of Possession Is a Disease with Them (1972)
Vietnam: The Struggle for Peace, 1972–1973 (1973)
The American Future: New Visions Beyond Old Frontiers (1980, 1999)
Reunion: A Memoir (1988)
The Lost Gospel of the Earth: A Call for Renewing Nature, Spirit and Politics
    (1996)
Irish Hunger: Personal Reflections on the Legacy of Famine (1998)
The Zapatista Reader (2001)
Irish on the Inside: In Search of the Soul of Irish America (2003)
The Port Huron Statement: The Visionary Call of the 1960s Revolution (2005)
Radical Nomad: C. Wright Mills and His Times (2006)
Street Wars: Gangs and the Future of Violence (2006)
Ending the War in Iraq (2007)
Voices of the Chicago 8: A Generation on Trial (2008)
Writings for a Democratic Society: The Tom Hayden Reader (2008)
The Long Sixties: From 1960 to Barack Obama (2009)
*Inspiring Participatory Democracy: Student Movements from Port Huron
    to Today* (2012)
Listen, Yankee! Why Cuba Matters (2015)

HELL NO

THE FORGOTTEN POWER OF THE VIETNAM PEACE MOVEMENT

TOM HAYDEN

Yale

UNIVERSITY PRESS

NEW HAVEN AND LONDON

Published with assistance from the foundation established in memory of Calvin Chapin of the Class of 1788, Yale College.

The author is grateful to *The Nation* magazine, where a portion of this book appeared, in slightly different form, in the issue of March 10, 2008, under the title "The Old Revolutionaries of Vietnam."

Yale University Press books may be purchased in quantity for educational, business, or promotional use. For information, please e-mail sales.press@yale.edu (U.S. office) or sales@yaleup.co.uk (U.K. office).

Set in Electra type by Tseng Information Systems, Inc.
Printed in the United States of America.

Library of Congress Control Number: 2016951994
ISBN: 978-0-300-21867-1 (hardcover : alk. paper)

A catalogue record for this book is available from the British Library.

This paper meets the requirements of ANSI/NISO Z39.48-1992 (Permanence of Paper).

10 9 8 7 6 5 4 3 2 1

To the millions who protested the Vietnam War.
Long live their memory.

Contents

Introduction

O
N JANUARY 13, 2015, I drove from our nation's capital across its historic bridges to a cold parking lot at Fort Myers, Virginia, where I felt jarred at seeing the vast hillside of solemn gravestones honoring those Americans who had sacrificed everything in our nation's wars, including fifty-eight thousand who perished in Vietnam, Laos, and Cambodia. I had visited Arlington many times before, helping kids find a sign of their grandfathers, sitting by Bobby Kennedy's simple cross, or taking in the John Kennedy memorial site with its eternal flame. I had been to Maya Lin's Vietnam Veterans Memorial wall many times as well, a gleaming black gash in the green earth surrounded by long and quiet lines of veterans, their families, and countless people who needed a connection, perhaps a catharsis, with lost soldiers they had known, or maybe were being touched by for the first time. Being there, surrounded by huge memorials to victims of other assassinations, espe-

cially the monuments to Dr. Martin Luther King Jr. and Abraham Lincoln, made me feel grounded in grief.

But I could not linger as long as I would have liked. I was here to talk to the Pentagon. With me was David Cortright, who had been an active-duty soldier in 1968–69 at Fort Hamilton, and who chose to oppose the Vietnam War and to organize GIs. Growing up a son of the Midwest Catholic working class he, like me, had no previous political involvements. He was now the director of Policy Studies at Notre Dame's Kroc Institute for International Peace Studies and the author of the definitive history *Soldiers in Revolt: GI Resistance During the Vietnam War*. David was our leader in initiating this attempt at honest dialogue with the Pentagon. His associate Terry Provance, an ordained minister with the United Church of Christ and lifelong peace activist, cleared our way into the building. We were joined by John McAuliff, long affiliated with the Quaker-inspired American Friends Service Committee and now a leading figure in peace and reconciliation efforts between the United States, Vietnam, and Cuba, and by Margery Tabankin, who grew up in the Weequahic neighborhood on the white suburban border of the Newark ghetto where I, in 1967, knocked on poor people's doors with the Newark Community Union Project, sponsored by Students for a Democratic Society (SDS). She had migrated to the Madison campus of the University of Wisconsin during a time of mass antiwar confrontations. Both of us were on accelerating learning curves: she went from student government to the presidency of the National Student Association, whose mandate at the time was to sever its hidden connection to the

CIA that had just been exposed by *Ramparts* magazine. Later she would spend years learning the politics of solidarity movements, political campaigns, lobbying Congress, and building broader coalitions with Democrats, feminists, and the clergy, until the day the Contra Wars in Nicaragua ended and the Sandinistas won their first national election. She went on to found the Hollywood Women's Political Action Committee with Jane Fonda, Barbra Streisand, Paula Weinstein, Marilyn Bergman, and many others, raising money and publicity for countless Democratic candidates and progressive causes. Also joining us that day was Heather Booth, a successful organizer and trainer of new organizers over the past fifty years. In the wings to report any newsworthy developments was Ira Arlook of Fenton Communications.

Precisely on time, we walked through the doors of Fort Myers Communications Center Building 405, entering a hallway full of soldiers coming and going, playing video games, reading, and hanging out. We were greeted by the Pentagon team, led by retired colonel Mark Franklin, chief of the History and Legacy Branch at the Pentagon's Vietnam Commemoration office, a crisp, buttoned-down veteran of three decades of military and policy experience, mainly in Korea. With him was Phil Waite, a communications specialist, and the affable former war correspondent Joseph Galloway, the kind of guy you could swap stories with all day. Joe had spent many years reporting from Vietnam and written the best-selling *We Were Soldiers Once . . . and Young*, coauthored with Lieutenant General Harold Moore, about the 1965 battle in Vietnam's Ia Drang Valley. Now, Joe was involved in a project to document the lives of Vietnam vets on tape. It was a massive undertaking and the challenge was daunting. Of 9 million Vietnam veterans, he said, 6 million had already passed away, and the losses were accelerating as time passed. Marge Tabankin immediately offered to help raise funds and open Hollywood doors to expedite Galloway's project.

We started by telling our personal stories and expectations for the meeting. I shared a story more personal than political. Since everyone knew of my activities during the Vietnam War—my unauthorized trips to Hanoi to seek the release of American POWs, my marriage to Jane Fonda, my trials in Chicago for helping to organize protests at the 1968 Democratic Party Convention—I simply said that all the stories of my efforts to end the war were true. I said my father, a World War II Marine, had disowned me for sixteen years, cutting me off from my younger sister, all because of what he read in the papers about my adventures. My mother had virtually lived in hiding every time my name was in the news.

I described my experience when I was hauled into a New York induction center: all I recall seeing was a room full of confused, fearful, and naked eighteen-year-olds like me. (I was finally classified 1-Y, which meant that I would be called to combat only in a dire national emergency—if, say, the Communists were landing on the beaches of San Diego.) I explained that torment and breakups had occurred in the families of soldiers, veterans, and political radicals alike. We were a generation divided by Big Lies and propaganda, although many had finally achieved reconciliation on personal levels.

We wanted now to honor Vietnam veterans for their sac-

rifice and suffering, including the many thousands who had
created an unprecedented GI peace movement and led the
effort to end the war. We believed we must put a stop to false
and sanitized history; real truth and sharing of stories were
crucial to any authentic reconciliation. We had learned, almost accidentally, that the Pentagon was embarked on a con-
gressionally mandated and funded effort to commemorate
the fiftieth anniversary of the war's escalation in 1965 when
the first combat troops were sent to Vietnam. Already Mark
Franklin and his team had posted an "interactive timeline" on
the Internet. It seemed, on its face, to be a *den* of denial, glossing over some events of the past and cherry-picking others
to highlight. Under the guise of honoring veterans and their
service, the timeline presented a distorted version of reality
and seemed more an exercise in propaganda than an honest
attempt to grapple with a complicated and disobliging historical record.

For example, the July 1, 1968, entry referred to the notorious Phoenix Program only by its goal to "break Vietcong support in the countryside." It omitted to mention that the program relied on systematic torture and assassination and that it
was shut down after media exposure and congressional hearings. Perhaps one shouldn't be surprised. After all, the program is extolled in today's *Army and Marine Counterinsurgency Manual* and by Lieutenant Colonel David Kilcullen, a
former top advisor to disgraced general David Petraeus, who
calls for "a global Phoenix Program" in the "war against terror."

The June 13, 1971, entry described the Pentagon Papers as
"leaked government memos written by government officials

that tell the story of U.S. policy." The characterization was at best banal and at worst neglected what was most significant about the whole affair, which ruptured government secrecy by exposing the deliberate and long-standing practice of both the White House and the Pentagon to confuse and mislead the American people about the war. Nowhere did the timeline acknowledge that the Nixon administration had failed in its attempt to convict Daniel Ellsberg and Anthony Russo, who had leaked the papers to the *New York Times* and the *Washington Post*, of espionage. The Pentagon Papers were important because they suggested that our critique of the war was right, or at least that those of us who had long opposed our government's deepening disaster in Indochina weren't wrong. The government's own documents proved it. Of all this, however, the Pentagon's 2014 timeline said not a word—perhaps because the state by its nature cannot accept blame, especially top governing military.

The timeline consigned public opposition to the war to just three demonstrations in 1969–70. There were no entries describing draft resistance, opposition among GIs, deserters to Canada and other countries, prayer vigils, the organization of moratoriums, letters written to Congress, civil disobedience, peace campaigns for Congress and the presidency, massive teach-ins, and so on.

We were mindful that former Republican senator and current defense secretary Chuck Hagel had said at the Vietnam Memorial that Americans had a duty "to be honest in our telling of history. There is nothing to be gained by glossing over the darker portions of a war, the Vietnam War that bitterly divided America. We must learn from our past mistakes, because that is how we avoid repeating past mistakes." Secretary of State John Kerry, a battle-tested Vietnam combat veteran who had served as a Swift Boat skipper patrolling the Mekong River and who later came to prominence opposing the war, had also chosen the road to reconciliation, playing a key role with Senator John McCain, a former POW, in forging the historic mutual recognition between the United States and Vietnam in 1995. Kerry said in Hanoi on August 7, 2015, in a ceremony marking twenty years of normalized relations, "We have the ability to overcome great bitterness and to substitute trust for suspicion and replace enmity with respect."

It was with such hopes that we had arranged to meet with Mark Franklin and his colleagues at the Pentagon. Our first obligation was to history and its tangled truths, so David Cortright was blunt when he said: "Your Vietnam narrative simply can't stand up to public scrutiny." Franklin said he was heartened that we, too, wanted to honor the sacrifice of the veterans. A sense of relief washed over the room. His mission was for the vets and vets only, though he himself was far from a dove. He invited us to collaborate on revising the website by the inclusion of Vietnam scholars we would help to select. There were many truths about Vietnam, he conceded, acknowledging the impact of the peace movement. Galloway added that, like the broader movement, Vietnam veterans who had opposed the war also had factions.

Franklin had evidently come prepared to move forward immediately, offering to set up that very afternoon a meeting for us with the leaders of the nonprofit Vietnam Veterans

Memorial Fund. No sooner was the offer made than the fund president, Jim Knotts, entered the room with a young aide, Reema Ghazi, the fund's education specialist. The website as well as its timeline, we were assured, was only in draft form.

Congress, however, had approved the project seven years before. The design was all but done. We were told that ultimately the website would include a "wall of faces of every lost soldier" and a display of every item left at the Vietnam Memorial wall (there were already four hundred thousand). There also would be some sort of revised version of the Pentagon's timeline. The peace movement's efforts to end the war would be included somewhere. But how? Clearly, progressive members of Congress and veterans of the vast opposition to the war would have to race to achieve inclusion, at much expense of time and energy. We realized that our fight over memory had just begun. The scales were tipped, but we had experience with flipping stories, from the underground press's coverage of the My Lai massacre to coverage of the Pentagon Papers in the *New York Times*. Experience showed how activism, combined with critical thinkers and news media funded by our donations or foundation grants, could put projects of historical reclamation and protest on a faster track. And now, with the advent of social media, we had a new edge, the potential power to dramatically and publicly expose the false stories that had circulated from the 1950s to the Obama presidency, and to cast into sharper relief the pivotal role that our protests had played.

In the time we had for back-and-forth we learned that the music being considered to accompany the timeline might include both Sergeant Barry Sadler's "Ballad of the Green Berets" and Edwin Starr's "War," with commentary. But where, we wondered, was Country Joe & the Fish's "I-Feel-Like-I'm-Fixin'-to-Die Rag" or Pete Seeger's "Where Have All the Flowers Gone" or John Fogerty's "Fortunate Son" or Crosby, Stills, Nash & Young's "Ohio" and "Find the Cost of Freedom"?

The history of the antiwar movement needed to be portrayed, including the crucial role of Vietnam Veterans Against the War. There would need to be inclusion and funding for women's experiences in war. We were assured that the official story would be revised with our input. "It's all eminently doable," Jim Knotts said.

What did that mean? At the least it meant that, organized properly, we could use the existing antiwar writings and the prodigious output of many books by scholars and eyewitnesses to wage a relentless battle for our memories to be respected. We would have to start with a small effort, just as the antiwar struggles began in 1965 before turning into one of the largest protest movements in American history. This task, like the original peace movement, would take years.

We needed to reclaim our history on a grand scale. Many players—members of Congress, including Barbara Lee, Jim McGovern, and several others, members of the clergy, foundations, liberal movements, and the new labor movement—would need to join together to plan this long campaign of historical reclamation, including developing a strategy of how to intervene once again in the telling of history. Storytellers, artists, actors, and musicians would need to be engaged in this effort. The more people were aroused, the more they might demand of Congress and the media, and the more the truth of history could be presented.

Some on the left would perhaps denounce the whole project—some already had. Some might want a memorial to anti-colonial and anti-imperialist movements, and an admission that Vietnam was never a "mistake" but a systemic genocidal program. And maybe such ideological positioning, brewed through bitterness and rage, is correct. Our movement, now as then, was divided with splits among radicals, revolutionaries, sectarians, moderates, and militants, including legions of paid FBI informants and provocateurs sent by our government. Disparate groups triggered a huge historic movement, but the war was finally ended by Vietnam veterans, the civil rights leadership, and a congressional bloc that woke up and took action. We should give credit and honor to the movement, however it splintered and burned out, because the broader struggle was a turning point in our history, notwithstanding all our mad, outrageous diversity. What we should honor and strive for today is an inclusive demonstration of the power of the peace movement.

There are liberal forces that may want to co-opt us, and conservative forces that surely want to erase us from history altogether. There are wealthy donors and hawkish neoconservatives who seek to use the example of Vietnam to escalate other wars everywhere and pursue endless campaigns of demonization against Islam to wipe out terrorism.

It is time for a new effort to reverse the propaganda about Vietnam and our movement to end the war. It is time for truth telling, for healing, and for legacy. Who will tell our story when we are gone? So much has already escaped memory, and now the time to capture remembrance is rapidly passing. We need to resist the military occupation of our minds. Long-defeated falsehoods are being resurrected again. As one example, the recent acclaimed film *Last Days of Vietnam* depicts the war as one of aggression: North Vietnam pointed a dagger of invasion to the South. That was the false claim of the State Department's White Paper that we debunked in 1965. Official history too often covers our truths in oblivion. The war makers seek to win on the battlefield of memory what they lost on the battlefields of war. Usually the victors write history; this time it is the losers who are deployed to do so. As long ago as 1979, Pulitzer Prize–winning journalist Frances FitzGerald warned in her book *America Revised* that the antiwar movement was disappearing from history textbooks which, she wrote, "contain no reference, or almost none, to the peace movement or to any of the political turmoil of the late sixties and early seventies . . . in the future, this slate may be wiped clean." That danger of historical cleansing has only increased, despite many subsequent excellent histories, films, and investigative reports. As FitzGerald feared, the mainstream impression is that "the war stopped because President Nixon and Secretary Kissinger decided that it should."

The Vietnam protest movement may never achieve the recognition already given other movements from the same era: civil rights, women's rights, farmworkers' rights, the environmental movement, and more recent struggles like that for LGBT rights. Earlier struggles for workers' rights in the 1930s were recognized, institutionalized, and legitimized in

American politics in ways the peace movement never has been. Even Barack Obama, a brilliant wordsmith, in *The Audacity of Hope* distanced himself from the sixties with sarcasm, writing, "Sometimes I felt as if I were watching the psychodrama of the Baby Boom generation, a tale rooted in old grudges and revenge plots hatched on a handful of college campuses long ago." Obama does credit "the Sixties Generation" with success in the admission of minorities and women into full citizenship, but the antiwar movement, including the role of Julian Bond, Dr. King, and the Vietnam Veterans Against the War, goes unmentioned. A movement that partly made Obama's achievement possible is stricken from the record he writes. Was it for political reasons? Obama certainly had to protect himself against the accusations his enemies made concerning his links to the Reverend Jeremiah Wright and "palling around with terrorists," as 2008 Republican vice presidential candidate Sarah Palin put it.

It was not until his historic victory night in November 2008, celebrated in a massive gathering in Grant Park, scene of the police riot at the 1968 Democratic National Convention, that David Axelrod, Obama's campaign manager, wrote in a personal note that the choice of Grant Park was a "conscious decision" because Obama and his advisors "wanted to symbolically overcome the damage that had been done to American idealism forty years before in Grant Park, Memphis and Los Angeles." Obama has never elaborated further.

Since there is today virtually no popular, activist, well-funded, and permanent peace movement, our recognition of such powerful grassroots groups is fading away into legend, banished to the musty bookcases of the Left. To be sure, groups like Peace Action, the Quakers, or the Institute for Policy Studies thrived during the nuclear-freeze campaign of the early eighties or the Iraq invasion of 2003–8, but their influence rapidly declined when the Cold War ended or the troops were pulled out. To avoid the consequences of negative public opinion, Washington launched secret drone wars as an alternative to sending American troops and thereby lessening casualties. On a much smaller scale than Vietnam, peace groups have mounted feisty opposition, exposed the secret manipulation of data, and driven the White House to a constant attempt to lessen civilian casualties. The passion and resilience of the peace movement flourish, despite the government's frantic effort to conceal information. Nevertheless, the key reason for the drones—the avoidance of American ground troops in yet another war—demonstrates the power of the Vietnam memory and represents a major achievement for a peace movement fifty years after American soldiers fled Saigon. A political worry about drafting and deploying American troops is one of the peace movement's most powerful and enduring legacies.

The neoconservatives, many of whom never served in Vietnam, nonetheless helped conceive and carry out a fifteen-year war in which 3 to 5 million Indochinese and fifty-eight thousand Americans were killed and many more suffered, only to have it all end in a historic American failure—and yet they have lived on to enjoy comfortable roles in successive administrations during a cycle of catastrophic wars. Few if any of the Vietnam pundits, elites, and sinking think tankers have apologized or resigned since Vietnam. Instead, they have risen in the ranks of the same national security establishment that oversaw the debacle of Vietnam while implementing further military follies based on many of the same assumptions that led to the Vietnam collapse. To take only one example, Bruce Reidel of the Brookings Institution, Obama's top advisor on terrorism, told the president, according to Bob Woodward's *Obama's Wars*, "Until we kill them, they're going to keep trying to kill us." There's diplomatic finesse and crisis management on full display! Meanwhile the spectrum of "legitimate" opinion has tilted to military options while marginalizing the voices of anyone with proven experience in the Vietnam peace movement.

The trivializing of the peace movement's history has distorted the public memory of Martin Luther King Jr., who opposed the Vietnam War in a speech in August 1965, a few months after the first SDS march on Washington. His most important antiwar orations, delivered in April 1967 at the Riverside Church in New York and at a mass rally in Central Park and before the United Nations, were met by angry editorials in the *New York Times* and the *Washington Post*, and condemned by the Johnson White House as well as by the leaders of labor and most civil rights organizations. It was inappropriate, they claimed, for a "Negro spokesman" to stray into the territory of foreign policy. And though King's antiwar message is included on the plaque at the King Memorial, he is generally remembered today as a civil rights leader, not a man who opposed the Vietnam War and was organizing a Poor People's Campaign until his last breath. The myth persists that freedom can be expanded at home while repression is imposed and massive bombings escalate abroad. Few remember that shortly after Dr. King's death, amid the police brutality and street battles at the 1968 Democratic National Convention, a mule train of civil rights workers from King's organization was there in silent tribute to what might have been. We were part of the cause he led, and he was part of us. History has shown he was right, for the full realization of his justice agenda is still blocked by the permanent war economy and national surveillance state.

One can only guess why so many elites want to forget the Vietnam peace movement by history cleansing, why public memories have atrophied, and why there are few if any memorials to peace. The steady denial of our impact, the persistent caricatures of who we really were, the constant questioning of our patriotism, the snide suggestions that we offered no alternative but surrender to the Communist threat have cast a pall of illegitimacy over our memory and had a chilling effect on many journalists, peace dissenters, and the current generation of students today. Of course, one reason for this forgetting is that the Vietnam War was lost, a historical fact representatives of a self-proclaimed superpower can never acknowledge. Accepting defeat is simply not permissible.

It is more convenient to lay the blame on the peace movement, liberal media, dovish politicians at home, and so-called enemies within. For if the war rested on false assumptions, the deaths of fifty-eight thousand Americans and millions of Indochinese people might reasonably be blamed on a whole generation of American policy makers, intellectuals, and generals. Those at fault could never look the families of the dead in the eye. Imagine the grief and rage among those families. Resignations might be required. Instead, the antiwar movement has been ignored or scapegoated while those truly at fault have enjoyed decades of immunity.

Since the Vietnam War makers cannot accept responsibility or acknowledge the full truth, those who opposed the war are needed more than ever, now and tomorrow, to prevent the dimming of memory and to keep history from repeating. We must write our own history, tell our own story, and teach our lessons of Vietnam. I am neither a historian nor a scholar. All my life I've been a writer, organizer, and activist. The reflections in this essay are one man's modest contribution to making sense of half a century of struggle for justice and dignity, peace and democracy. We need to understand better why we did what we did and what it meant, not only for those of us who lived and helped to make this history, but also to tease out for the generations to come what lessons might be learned from the legacy that these great upheavals left us. Of one lesson I have no doubt: peace and justice movements can make a difference.

It is true that our movement was deeply fragmented and rarely unified. The antiwar movement reproduced many of the racial, class, gender, and cultural divides of the society from which we came. On top of those differences there crept the infection of sectarian power struggles that still afflicts social movements in general. Thousands of informants and COINTELPRO (the notorious FBI counterintelligence program) provocateurs did their best to spread the poisons of distrust, division, and violence. Without unity, how could a common story be told to future generations?

It is not too late to recover and begin again. This is already happening in the reconciliation process between the Vietnamese and our country. But we must not forget that for the Vietnamese, the war is not fully over. The soil of Vietnam is contaminated with Agent Orange. Unexploded ordnance covers the landscape. Those deformed by our defoliants will transmit their disabilities to their children for generations. Each generation of Americans has a responsibility to help mitigate this permanent damage. And yet, by the tens of thousands, American veterans and their families are touring old battlefields, shaking hands, and sharing tea with their old enemies. The sentiments of resolution are palpable. So are the feelings experienced by visitors to the Vietnam Veterans Memorial in Washington, DC.

The disaster that began in Vietnam still spirals on as a conflict between empire and democracy. The cycle of war continues its familiar path. Truth, it is said, is war's first casualty. Memory is its second.

1

THE ERA OF PROTEST against the Vietnam War
was unique; from it emerged a nationwide peace
movement on a scale never before seen in American history. There had been previous war resisters—for example, the Society of Friends (Quakers), the
opponents of the Mexican War and the Indian wars, critics
of the imperial taking of Cuba, Puerto Rico, and the Philippines, and objectors to World War I—numbering in the many
thousands. But no peace movement had ever been as large
scale, long lasting, intense, and threatening to the status quo
as the protests against the Vietnam War.

The roots of the Vietnam peace movement were in the
civil rights, student, and women's movements of the early sixties. The civil rights movement inspired the National Organization for Women and Women's Strike for Peace, which
opposed Strontium-90 and pushed for President John F. Kennedy's 1963 Test Ban Treaty with the Soviet Union. Together
these movements were demanding a shift from Cold War priorities to "jobs and justice," the banner of the 1963 March
on Washington. Adherents of these movements were deeply
shocked by the assassination of President Kennedy on November 22, 1963, and appalled by the subsequent escalation in

Vietnam. The Student Nonviolent Coordinating Committee's (SNCC) Mississippi Summer Project to register black voters and the Mississippi Freedom Democratic Party's convention challenge in Atlanta occurred at the time of the August 1964 Tonkin Gulf "incident" and war authorization. Students for a Democratic Society (SDS) supported a policy of going "part of the way" with LBJ in late 1964 while planning the first peace march for April 1965 in case President Johnson broke his pledge to deploy no ground troops. The Free Speech Movement on the campus of the University of California at Berkeley in September 1964 set the stage for the Vietnam Day Committee and Berkeley's first teach-in in May 1965. SNCC, SDS, the Free Speech Movement, the Chicano civil rights movement, the Puerto Rican movement, and the National Organization for Women all were asserting domestic demands just as the U.S. draft and troop escalation took place in early 1965.

During the Vietnam peace movement era, Americans took to the streets in numbers exceeding one hundred thousand on at least a dozen occasions, sometimes reaching half a million. At least twenty-nine young Americans were killed while protesting the war. Tens of thousands were arrested. The greatest student strike in American history shut down campuses for weeks. Black people rose in hundreds of urban rebellions inspired partly by the shift from the War on Poverty to the Vietnam War. GIs rebelled on scores of bases and ships, some refused orders, others threw their medals on the steps of Congress, and a few attacked their superior officers, prompting warnings about the actual "collapse" of the armed forces by the seventies. Significant peace candidates appeared in congressional races by 1966 and became a significant force in presidential politics by 1968. President Johnson was forced to renounce his reelection hopes because of a revolt within his own party in 1968, and his successor, Richard Nixon, would ultimately resign after escalating a secret war and unleashing spies and provocateurs against dissenters at home.

The 1965–75 peace movement reached a scale that threatened the foundations of the American social order, making it both an inspirational model for future social movements and a nightmarish narrative that our governing elites have tried to wipe from collective memory ever since. It's far simpler, after all, to incorporate into the American national story a tale about movements that triumphed over racial hatred, lynching, genocide, and the burning of "witches" than it is to admit the inglorious saga of a failed war in which tens of thousands of Americans died while killing millions of people in a faraway land.

The events of those ten years between 1965 and 1975 might be compared to the "general strike," or noncooperation of the slaves on southern plantations that undermined the Confederacy. As W. E. B. DuBois put it in 1935 in his classic *Black Reconstruction*, "The slave entered upon a general strike against slavery by the same methods that he had used during the period of the fugitive slave. He ran away to the first place of safety and offered his services to the Federal Army . . . and so it was true that this withdrawal and bestowal of his labor decided the war."

In a similar manner, the twentieth-century Vietnamese

peasants demanding land reform under the French colonialists might be likened to the nineteenth-century African slaves who resisted slavery and demanded "forty acres and a mule." The role of the Vietnamese against their French and American occupiers was key. By 1970, the Vietnamese resistance to the American imperium would ultimately prompt a de facto general strike in America that paralyzed campuses, cities, and barracks, forcing a realignment in American politics and bringing the war to its end.

The first stirrings of the American resistance began in college or university communities with polite dissent and educational teach-ins in 1964. By 1969 and 1970 there was a wave of student strikes that shuttered hundreds of campuses, involved more than 4 million in protests, and forced closures of key institutions through the spring semester in 1970, according to Kirkpatrick Sale in his authoritative history *SDS*. "There were major campus demonstrations at the rate of more than a hundred a day, students at a total of at least 350 institutions went out on strike and 536 schools were shut down completely for some period of time, 51 of them for the entire year." At the same time, from 1964 through 1971, there were seven hundred "civil disturbances" with more than one hundred deaths in Watts, Newark, and Detroit alone. Those "riots" were in protest against budgets favoring war spending over social programs, and they included many returning Vietnam veterans or their family members at home. There also came a significant GI revolt that, as chronicled by Lawrence Baskir and William Strauss in *Chance and Circumstance: The Draft, the War and the Vietnam Generation*, saw more than five hundred "fraggings" (attacks by soldiers against their own officers using fragmentation grenades) in 1969 and 1970, scores of "riots" on military bases, forty thousand desertions to Canada and Sweden, and official reports that the armed forces themselves were "approaching collapse." According to historian Jonathan Neale in his *A People's History of the Vietnam War*, "From 1970 on, the fight against the war was moving from the campus to the barracks."

Amid this general collapse, the peace movement was able to generate a political constituency that attracted political candidates who threatened the Cold War consensus. The political revolt began in Massachusetts in 1962 with H. Stuart Hughes's independent run for the state senate, and then became a real political insurgency in California in 1966 with the Robert Scheer and Stanley Sheinbaum candidacies in Democratic congressional primaries. Those energetic efforts, in turn, helped prompt the national presidential campaigns of Senators Eugene McCarthy and Robert Kennedy in 1968 and Senator George McGovern in 1972. The McCarthy campaign was driven almost entirely by student volunteers, who later created the massive Vietnam moratoriums. A possible victory for peace was lost when Robert Kennedy was assassinated in June 1968 shortly after the killing of Martin Luther King Jr. in April. By 1972, the Democratic Party had adopted a platform calling for complete and immediate withdrawal from Vietnam. The military draft was ended in January 1973, thus relieving millions of young men from the fear of being conscripted to fight and possibly to die in an increasingly unpopular war.

American politics would be changed for decades by the anti-Vietnam revolt, much as the abolitionists and Radical Republicans, allied with the Underground Railroad and the general strike by slaves, helped to turn the tide of the Civil War. The killings of King and the Kennedys, like the assassination of Lincoln a century before, undermined the transformative possibilities of a second Reconstruction. The first Reconstruction anticipated the Student Nonviolent Coordinating Committee one hundred years later with its freedom schools, literacy projects, economic demands for "forty acres and a mule," voter registration, and election of twenty emancipated black men to the U.S. House of Representatives, two to the U.S. Senate, six hundred to state assemblies, and fourteen hundred to other elective offices across the South. All was destroyed in the racist backlash known as Jim Crow. That remarkable story of reaction and betrayal is well told by Eric Foner in his great histories of Reconstruction.

Fifty years later, I still felt stunned when Clayborne "Clay" Carson, the Stanford historian, presented a paper at a gathering describing the movement of southern sharecroppers, the SNCC core constituency, as part of "the anti-colonial agrarian reform movements" sweeping the world from then to now, whether in Selma, South Vietnam, southern Africa, or, for that matter, Russia in the era of Alexander II, who abolished serfdom in 1861.

By "general strike" I do not mean a planned or coordinated campaign, nor one led by radical vanguards, but rather a widespread refusal on the part of vast numbers of people to any longer take part in the usual habits of daily life, instead withdrawing their participation in the regnant political culture all at once for an extended period of time. This sort of phenomenon requires a level of desperation and evinces a massive discontent much more spontaneous than controlled as part of a general disintegration of the status quo. Recent examples include Tunisia in 2010 or the half million immigrants who gathered peaceably in downtown Los Angeles on March 25, 2006, with similar protests in one hundred other American cities. The Los Angeles immigrant outpouring came after months of planning in which immigrant activists and labor unions were predicting its ranks would reach only twenty-five thousand—at best, fifty thousand. The Arab Spring in Tunisia began on December 17, 2010, because Mohamed Bouazizi, a street vendor, immolated himself in protest. Occupy Wall Street began when a handful of disenfranchised people sat down in a circle to discuss what they really wanted to do.

Of course, organizing is important in the long buildup of prior movements and past experiences of victory and defeat, but there always seems to be an unpredicted moment when a new chapter of social movement history begins. Activist peace and justice groups gave inspiration and support to this Great Refusal to conform during Vietnam, but widespread discontent, even desperation, caused by the draft, body bags, and photos of napalmed peasants and children were the motor forces. According to the blue-ribbon Scranton Commission on Campus Unrest appointed by President Nixon after the May 1970 Kent State killings of four students, "The crisis on American campuses has no parallel in the history of this nation. This crisis has roots in divisions of American society as deep as any since the Civil War. If this trend continues, if this crisis of understanding endures, the very survival of the nation will be threatened."

The crisis threatened the stability of the economic system, too. As Thomas Powers observed in his book *Vietnam: The War at Home*, "New York's financial community and the interests it represented were seriously worried about the war" and its toll in budget deficits and Great Society programs as early as 1967. That same year, a business-oriented group, Executives for Peace, started placing full-page antiwar ads in the *New York Times*.

There was no light at either end of the tunnel, from Berkeley to Saigon. The war and the growing crisis at home had split the unity of the Cold War Establishment, revealed most sharply in the Watergate crisis when Nixon chose to circumvent the Constitution in order to prolong the war. It was in this context that the hawkish ex-Marine Daniel Ellsberg, along with Anthony Russo, his co-conspirator, chose to leak the secret Pentagon Papers and face espionage charges.

The April 1965 SDS march on Washington against the Vietnam War was the largest peace march in American history. It was a small march by today's standards, only about twenty-five thousand strong. Five years later there were hundreds of thousands at moratoriums and mobilizations. The lesson we learned was that we had to keep marching and mobilizing and expanding our base again and again. Paul Potter of SDS, Bob Moses of SNCC, and Staughton Lynd, a radical sociologist and historian, all addressed the crowd. Paul's speech was the most memorable. Just twenty-five years old, he spoke for a new generation:

> Most of us grew up thinking that the United States was a strong but humble nation. . . . What in fact has the war done for freedom in America? It has led to even more vigorous government efforts to control information, manipulate the press and pressure and persuade the public through distorted or downright dishonest documents like the White House White Paper. . . .
>
> This is an unusual march because the large majority of us here are not involved in a peace movement as their primary basis of concern. . . . What kind of system is this? We must name the system, name it, describe it, analyze it, understand it and change it.

Many in the crowd already thought they "knew" the system included capitalism or imperialism. But Paul was an original thinker who sensed new realities could not be contained in old labels without activists eventually turning into dogmatists. Those questions continue to be debated today. They are worthy of serious consideration. But that's not who we were. Paul Potter was dropping out of the university to become a community organizer in Cleveland, working mostly with welfare mothers and reading through his nights.

I participated in the march from backstage. We brought a busload of poor black people from Newark so they might observe and march with the rest of the movement as they chose. As the sun went down over the National Mall, we drove back to Newark's precincts and parishes of the poor.

In November, Carl Oglesby, another eloquent SDS intellectual, would brilliantly call the system "corporate liberalism." That name seemed to explain the role of Democratic Party liberals who were supporting and voting for the war, and opened a sharp difference between the more radical and more pragmatic perspectives in two short years.

Meanwhile, everything grew worse. By December 1965 the number of dead American soldiers had climbed to 1,928, Saigon army casualties were 11,242, and North Vietnamese casualties were unknown. The draft became a life-and-death personal question for thousands of students that year, and the early steps toward Selective Service resistance were beginning.

There was another ominous change. The Haight-Ashbury district of San Francisco was flooded with LSD. Some suspected that the upsurge in such drugs was the work of the CIA, which had, after all, deliberately sponsored and profited from much of the heroin trafficking in Indochina. The agency had failed to suppress Alfred W. McCoy's exposé, *The Politics of Heroin,* of CIA complicity in the Indochinese drug trade. We from Newark were moving to the Bay Area, finding crash pads for scores upon scores of "hippies," a shorthand tag created by the mass media and employed as a cultural cudgel to split our generation between "straights" and "longhairs," including our soldiers in their bases and barracks.

When the "corporate liberals" — more accurately, the new doves in the ruling institutions — began to demand disengagement for national security and economic reforms, their views converged with the new peace movement to erode critical support for the Vietnam policy. People power had undermined the pillars of that policy: public opinion, the military draft, and an affordable budget for war. The democratic process was prevailing over the "cancer on the presidency," as White House counsel John Dean described the Watergate scandal in 1973. In the eyes of many Establishment figures who originally endorsed the war, it had become unwinnable, unaffordable, and a threat to domestic tranquility, especially because of the peace movement. They were widely, if discreetly, known as the "Wise Men," their tale well recounted by Walter Isaacson and Evan Thomas in their 1986 book, *The Wise Men: Six Friends and the World They Made*. At the center was Averell Harriman (whose fortune came from the Union Pacific and Southern Pacific railroads and Wells Fargo), who was New York governor before becoming the special ambassador to the United States–Vietnam peace talks. I first met him a day or two after the assassination of Dr. Martin Luther King Jr. as Washington was burning outside the windows of his spacious office. Harriman was having birthday cake as I tried to brief him on the Paris peace talks.

The other Wise Men and others in their circle were former secretary of state Dean Acheson, former secretary of defense Robert Lovett, former ambassadors to the Soviet Union George Kennan and Charles "Chip" Bohlen, secretary of defense Clark Clifford, Henry Kissinger from Harvard University, and John J. McCloy, who had been president of the World Bank, chairman of Chase Manhattan Bank, the Ford Foundation, and the Council on Foreign Relations. They were at the pinnacle of the power elite.

Concern about losing Vietnam and perhaps America became their growing concern as they met to brief Johnson in the White House. Pending was a Pentagon demand to call up 208,000 new American troops. One official said, "Essentially, we are fighting Vietnam's birth rate." Inflation was growing. The cities were burning, the campuses convulsed by strikes, the soldiers deeply disturbed, even angry. The Tet Offensive was being promoted as a great victory for the United States even though it had nearly provoked a complete collapse of power and morale in Saigon. As they sipped coffee in the Oval Office with the president, the Wise Men summoned the nerve to tell Lyndon Johnson he couldn't win the war and that he had to disengage. According to Isaacson and Thomas, LBJ's first reaction, typical of the powerful, was "Who the hell brainwashed those friends of yours?" "I smelled a rat," National Security Advisor Walt W. Rostow later said. "It was a put-up job," meaning he believed someone among the Wise Men was pushing to end the war.

Nevertheless, LBJ was forced to abandon his bid for re-election that spring, although he continued to look for ways to restore himself to power and win the war. I could not then imagine the drawn-out struggles that lay ahead—struggles that would lead to the B-52 Christmas bombings of Hanoi in December 1972 and, two years later, to a presidential resignation amid a hurricane of public protest at high crimes and misdemeanors and under the shadow of a likely impeachment.

The peace movement has sometimes been stereotyped in blurry and incoherent images of campus chaos, potheads, and New Age prophets, but in truth the core of its membership unfolded with an inner logic: drawn first from the margins of society among young people who could be drafted but could not vote; then from the inner cities where African Americans and Latinos were drafted in great numbers; then from poets and intellectuals; and finally spreading into mainstream political sectors considered centrist. The acceleration of protest in the two years from 1965 to 1967 was rapid. The peace constituency became vast enough to polarize American politics with the adoption of an inside-outside strategy, moratoriums combined with elections, causing the Democratic Party to realign itself between 1966 and 1968. The Republican and Pentagon countermovement was vicious, ranging from police repression to Nixon's "dirty tricks" campaign to false promises of peace to sway voters and finally to the withdrawal of U.S. ground troops combined with an invisible air war. The war ended nonetheless, politically with the fall of Nixon at Watergate and on the battlefield with the fall of Saigon.

The Vietnam peace movement, however, was so divided by counterintelligence programs and our own internal power struggles and sectarian feuds that it was impossible ever to cohere into a united national force, unlike the AFL-CIO or NAACP, two organizations that had managed to overcome their internal strife.

We were riven by internal divisions along the lines of class, race, and gender; civilian resisters and rebels within the military; street protestors and politicians; advocates of nonviolence, electoral politics, disruption, and resistance. These different factions often quarreled bitterly, some at the instigation of the FBI but also due to ego or sectarian and ideological rivalries among our ranks.

Still, we managed to come together in cumulative creative ways that brought the war to an end, and with it the demise of various other antiwar groupings. For example, students pushed their professors to mount teach-ins, which were denounced by many as too tepid an approach. But the same teach-ins reached and awakened, even radicalized, a much larger base of fence-sitting students. Similarly, the growing draft resistance helped prompt political leaders like Senators McCarthy, McGovern, and Kennedy to define their campaigns in large part as acceptable alternatives to the radical confrontations, even using phrases like "Clean for Gene" to distinguish themselves from the hippies.

In the end, moderate sectors of the Establishment joined with the pragmatic wing of the peace and justice movements to disengage from Vietnam in order to save the stability of the American system as a whole. (I explored these dynamics in considerable detail in my book *The Long Sixties: From 1960 to Barack Obama*.) Averell Harriman even became the chairman of the first Vietnam moratorium of October 15, 1969. Marching veterans, feminists, gays and lesbians, rank-and-file Democrats, and students gave birth to the notion of a "rainbow coalition," challenging Nixon's strategy of manipulating the "silent majority."

The tragedy of the antiwar movement was that the whole never grew to become greater than its parts. It might have been unified from 1968 onward if Martin Luther King Jr. had lived, if Robert Kennedy had been elected president, and if the war had terminated in 1969. That possibility was destroyed by their assassinations, leaving a disoriented, scarred, and scattered generation. When the war did finally end in 1975, many of its opponents had drifted away from national activism and moved on with their lives, or taken up more promising personal quests and local agendas. The peace movement had exhausted its historic role without a general recognition—even among ourselves—that we had made history. Instead, many of us saw defeat where there had been victory.

2

W E WERE YOUNG, in our early twenties, and we were required to learn about Vietnam intellectually, on our own, not from dogma, and construct an alternative to the dominant paradigm over our lives: that the Cold War was necessary to stop monolithic international Communism from knocking over the "dominoes" of the Free World, one by one. In our teach-ins, our readings, and writings by Carl Oglesby, Robert Scheer, and others, we drew our own conclusion that it was revolutionary nationalism, led by Communists, that the United States was opposing with military force and client dictatorships under the facade of the "Free World." With respect to the "aggression from the North" argument, we countered that Vietnam was a single nation divided only temporarily by the agreement that ended the French war at the 1954 Geneva Conference, and later had been denied the guarantee of a nationwide election, which Ho Chi Minh would have won, as even President Eisenhower conceded in his memoir, *Mandate for Change*. As reported in the March 8, 1965, *I. F. Stone's Weekly*, 80 percent of the National Liberation Front's weapons were captured from the United States or Saigon militaries, and the Pentagon's own charts showed only

179 Communist-made weapons were found among 15,100 captured by Saigon between 1962 and 1964.

The teach-ins were the participatory method of our exploration. The March 24, 1965, teach-in on the University of Michigan's Ann Arbor campus drew together thirty-three hundred students and faculty leaders in all-night discussions and lectures. The event was carried by national radio hookup for twelve hours and reached 122 campuses. The May 21–22, 1965, Berkeley teach-in on the campus of the University of California attracted thirty-five thousand participants over thirty-six hours.

The April 17, 1965, March on Washington was then the largest antiwar march in American history. That fall forty thousand were marching in Washington, twenty thousand in New York City, and fifteen thousand in Oakland. Thousands more marched in eighty other cities. From no draft protests in 1964, just three years later there were antidraft actions on half of all public university campuses. Three thousand young men signed "We Won't Go" petitions in the spring of 1967. Five thousand turned in their draft cards and some ten thousand to twenty-five thousand "delinquent cases" were reported to the U.S. Department of Justice between 1966 and 1969, according to Staughton Lynd and Michael Ferber's history, *The Resistance*. Ramsey Clark's Justice Department was prosecuting fifteen hundred draft refusal cases by 1968. The November 1969 National Moratorium was hailed as the "largest peace march ever," with half a million gathering in Washington alone. Over the course of that decade there were at least two national protests per year involving tens of thousands on each occasion.

Public opinion turned against the war much earlier than many historians concede. Conventional wisdom holds that, except for the liberal elite and the college crowd, Americans favored the Vietnam War until mid-1968. Only after CBS newsman Walter Cronkite gave up on the war did the public follow him. The data shows, however, that public opinion turned much earlier, and it both followed and led to the further growth of the peace movement. The Gallup polling organization asked one question consistently throughout the war: "In view of the developments since we entered the fighting in Vietnam, do you think the United States made a mistake sending troops to fight in Vietnam?" August 1968 was the first time the proportion of those answering "yes" crossed 50 percent for the first time. Decision makers in Washington, however, knew that what counts most is not percentages but emerging trends. Looked at this way, the crucial time was March–May 1966, just after Arkansas senator William Fulbright mesmerized the public with critical Senate hearings on Vietnam, faulting an "arrogance of power" as the root cause. The "mistake" response to the Gallup question jumped from 29 percent to 42 percent in just two months. In other words, within a year of President Johnson's military buildup in February 1965, the war was in big trouble with the public, and this factor was central in all subsequent decisions by Presidents Johnson, Nixon, and Ford.

The path was opened to electing peace candidates in future congressional races, among them Bob Kastenmeier (1964; he had first been elected in 1958), Bella Abzug (1970), Ron Dellums (1970), Pat Schroeder (1972), and Tom Harkin (1974), and in presidential primaries—Eugene McCarthy and Robert Kennedy (1968), and Shirley Chisholm and George McGovern (1972). In 1968 alone, one hundred peace candidates ran in twenty states—the same year that Lyndon Johnson was surrendering the presidency and peace forces were remaking the Democratic Party.

The assassinations of Martin Luther King and Robert Kennedy, coupled with sharp divisions among organized labor, Cold War Democrats, and the new peace and justice movements, made a presidential victory impossible in 1968. Thirty million Americans voted for the flawed campaign of George McGovern in 1972, a total inconceivable at the time of the first march only seven years before. Both the rank-and-file activists in the peace movement and the peace candidates who arose from the movement have to be considered together in weighing the immense impact generated from the margins to the mainstream between 1965 and 1968.

In the language of the Left, a domestic and global insurgency had driven open a "split in the ruling class" between those who favored "victory" at any cost and those who believed in cutting military, economic, and political losses in order to restore stability at home. It was not simply an argument among the powerful. The institutional order fractured. If not a "pre-revolutionary situation," the greatest domestic conflict since the Civil War and the Great Depression was precipitated. The growth and radicalization of the movement continued at a rapid pace not seen since the populist and radical labor movements of a century before.

Many universities were exposed by student research as being complicit in the war machine. The Voice student party in Ann Arbor, for example, discovered that the University of Michigan was developing infrared sensors for jungle warfare. Protests against Dow Chemical's production of napalm erupted on more than one hundred campuses. Universities began calling in the police, "marking the first time that outside force had ever been used on college campuses on such a large scale." The epithet *pig* first appeared in *New Left Notes* on September 25, 1967. Escalation of the war caused an escalation of resistance. There was, on all sides, an escalation of rhetoric, and the mood of the country coarsened and soured.

There were forty-one cases of bombing and arson in the fall of 1968, mainly against draft boards and ROTC buildings — quadruple the number of the spring before. In 1969 there were at least eighty-four bombings, attempted bombings, or arson attacks in the first six months alone. The numbers rose to 169 cases of bombing and arson in May 1969, and four ROTC buildings burned each day during a single week. All this was before the founding of the Weather Underground in 1970.

The state went to severe lengths to prosecute a war that a majority of Americans thought was a mistake. At least twenty-nine American college students were killed by police, troopers, guardsmen, or vigilantes while protesting against the war. Four died at Kent State, four in the Chicano Moratorium, and two at Jackson State. This count doesn't include the hundreds killed in black urban insurrections during those years, as black youth were conscripted for the front lines in Vietnam while funding for the War on Poverty was scaled back. These terrible numbers must include the eight Americans who took their own lives by self-immolation to protest the war: Alice Herz, Norman Morrison, Roger Allen LaPorte, Florence Beaumont, George Winne Jr., Hiroko Hayasaki, Eric Thoen, and Ronald Brazee.

We also must remember the counterinsurgency programs we faced at home. For example, Elizabeth Drew reported in the *Atlantic* in May 1969 that Johnson's deputy attorney general, Richard Kleindienst, recommended that war protestors be "rounded up and put in detention camps." The FBI assigned twenty thousand full-time agents to monitor the activities of protestors and, according to Kirkpatrick Sale, "at least an equal number of informers" and twenty federal agencies, including the U.S. Army, gathered "political dossiers on eighteen million civilians." Attorney Lewis F. Powell Jr., soon to be appointed to the Supreme Court, advocated mass expulsions: "The only language student extremists understand is force." During the Democratic Convention protests in Chicago of 1968, the FBI assigned 320 agents. The Pentagon established the Civil Disturbance Directorate to suppress campuses and ghettos. Prosecutors and grand juries pursued twenty "conspiracy" cases against antiwar defendants in Chicago, Seattle, Harrisburg, Gainesville, Boston, and beyond. Drug arrests of American teenagers jumped 774 percent from 1960 levels. The liberal *New York Times* editorialized in 1968, "The line has to be drawn somewhere if an orderly society is to survive." Having lectured Dr. King to stay in his place, the *Times* now called for the suppression of a new and more militant generation. By 1970, one national survey found that an estimated 1 million students described themselves as "revolutionaries."

Today, in 2017, all this is only dimly remembered and mostly through images of disorder and mayhem. Indeed, chaos is the chief cultural memory of the sixties, but not the actual "Operation Chaos" unleashed by our intelligence agencies against thousands of youthful resisters and such major figures as Muhammad Ali, Dr. Benjamin Spock, and John Lennon. Images of chaos smother the logical sequence of domestic radicalization and repression that could have been prevented at any time by a policy of de-escalation, negotiation, and American withdrawal, if Johnson and Nixon had been sincere in their promises of sending no American ground troops (1964) or "Peace is at hand" (1972). In the end, the democratic process did not override the will of the war makers until Richard Nixon was driven out of office and the Saigon regime collapsed. As Thomas Powers concluded in his 1973 study, *Vietnam: The War at Home*, "The anti-war movement in the United States created the necessary conditions for the shift in official policy from escalation to disengagement."

The thoroughgoing racism of the war is sometimes forgotten by the universal damning of the Vietnamese as "gooks." The Pulitzer Prize–winning author Viet Thanh Nguyen, born in Vietnam and raised in the United States, where he teaches at the University of Southern California, includes this jolting passage in his book, *Nothing Ever Dies: Vietnam and the Memory of War*: "Gooks do have feelings. . . . Having carried ourselves over, or been brought over, from the other side — we Gooks, we goo-goos, we slopes, we dinks, we zipperheads, we slant-eyes, we yellow ones, we brown ones, we Japs, we Chinks, we ragheads, we sand niggers, we Orientals, we who cannot be distinguished between ourselves because we all look alike—we know that the condition of our being and our self-representation is that we are both ourselves and others."

The binational, bilingual author compares his work to that of African Americans like Ralph Ellison or W. E. B. DuBois, both of whom wrote of invisibility or the paradox of double identity in a racist culture, a condition now being played out among Asian Americans. In a conversation I had with him in Los Angeles, he stressed the irony of those three hundred thousand South Vietnamese troops whose remains litter the battlefields where they died as part of a U.S. coalition that armed and trained them to the very end. They are not identified officially under U.S. law even today because doing so would qualify their families for death benefits. Similarly, the United States never paid the $7 billion promised to Vietnam under the Paris Peace Agreement. This inherent racism has roots in past Chinese occupations and French colonialism. Each time the deceased are forgotten, they are rendered dead again.

Neglected in most Vietnam narratives are three strands of resistance underlying the growth of the larger peace movement from 1965 to 1975. The first strand was Vietnam's anticolonial, nationalist resistance after World War II, which arose long before a peace movement elsewhere was on the horizon. In the conventional story, the role of the Vietnamese on political, military, and diplomatic battlefronts is rarely mentioned. It is crucial to recall it. The Viet Minh decided to take up prolonged armed struggle against their French overseers in relative isolation but in the belief their resistance eventually would provoke war weariness and an antiwar movement in France. They made a key distinction between the French government and the French people, a distinction that would carry over to the American war. Whether Confucian or Marxist, this Vietnamese approach meant fighting fiercely on the battlefield while framing the struggle in terms the French people might understand: the rights of self-determination and national independence, harking back to the ideals of the French Revolution. This same nationalist, patriotic approach attempted to unify Vietnamese of nearly all backgrounds in opposition to foreign colonial intervention.

The same strategy would be applied to the American war. From the beginning, then, theirs was a military struggle with core political and diplomatic dimensions. After World War II, the U.S. government had a fateful choice to make. It could have pursued coexistence with Vietnam's Communist-led nationalist front, the Viet Minh, led by Ho Chi Minh, or intervention with weapons and funds to restore white French colonial rule. For a brief period in 1945, operatives of the U.S. Office of Strategic Services (OSS), the forerunner of the Central Intelligence Agency, advised cooperating with the popular Viet Minh forces. Ho Chi Minh encouraged nonintervention by declaring Vietnam's national independence in language inspired by the American Declaration of Independence.

Eventually, however, the United States chose the path of shoring up the French because Vietnam would be a proxy in the Cold War the U.S. government was waging against its World War II Soviet ally. Since the majority of the Vietnamese population sympathized with Ho and the Viet Minh, the joint French-U.S. strategy inevitably became a dirty war with torture, mass detentions, civilian casualties, and iron-fisted rule, which gradually alienated much of the French population with its republican tradition.

Yet the Viet Minh defeated the French not in the salons or streets of France but militarily on the battlefield at Dien Bien Phu in 1954. There were right-wing plots by French military officers to replace the French regime. The government of Pierre Mendès-France finally negotiated a political settlement at Geneva in 1954 that outlined French troop withdrawals, a temporary partition of the country at the seventeenth parallel, and a plan for nationwide elections and reunification two years later. The Eisenhower administration, however, intervened to prevent elections and reunification, choosing instead to adopt the Korean War model of permanent partition into two Vietnams. That fateful decision guaranteed the gradual escalation of the U.S. war and the creation of a client regime in Saigon.

It also cemented a dark assumption that immoral means were necessary to defeat Communism and preserve the option of pro-Western market economies under friendly and compliant regimes. The immoral means were justified in part by a racial superiority complex toward "Orientals" as inherently inferior savages who were thought to place no value on individual life. General Curtis LeMay, President Kennedy's air force secretary, expressed it this way: "We ought to nuke the chinks." Or as Lyndon Johnson had so memorably put it, urging that the United States beef up its air force, "Without superior air power, America is a bound and throttled giant, impotent and easy prey to any yellow dwarf with a pocket knife." Mr. Kurtz, the central character of Joseph Conrad's imperishable novel, *Heart of Darkness*, set in Africa, put it best when he declared: "Exterminate the brutes!" Conrad perfectly understood the inherent cruelty and racism of the colonialist mentality, and his prescient book anticipates much that would deform the twentieth century, including our blunder in Vietnam.

Yet Robert M. Kaplan, in his introduction to a recent reissue of Conrad's masterpiece, derived precisely the wrong lesson from the novel, writing that "Vietnam, like Iraq, represented a war of frustrating half-measures against an enemy that respected no limits" and was "not limited by Western notions of war." He seemed convinced that, as the saying goes, had we taken the gloves off, victory would have been ours. The truth is that we dropped more tons of bombs on Indochina than we did on all the white Axis powers in World War II. The United States unleashed 7.8 million tons of bombs on Indochina compared with 2.7 million tons dropped by Allied forces. Such callous disregard for Asian lives was ubiquitous in our press of the time, with its frequent references to the Vietnamese or Chinese as "ants" or other insects, which suggested extermination as a solution.

Another development was the founding of the New Centurions, our Special Operations forces conceived as a detached fraternity of professional warriors disdainful of civilian voters, journalists, and politicians, and thus suspicious of democracy itself. In this view, wars were lost on the home front. The public was a potential enemy and democracy a process to be tolerated at best and circumvented when necessary.

The second strand of the deep antiwar movement was the growing resistance from communities of color, who linked their civil rights struggles to the cause of peace. The young civil rights leader Julian Bond published in 1967 one of the earliest illustrated books on Vietnam, a well-researched comic book aimed at young black men facing the draft. It showed the advanced perspective of some African American students in the early years of the Vietnam War. Bond wrote this early people's history, with illustrations by T. G. Lewis, the year after the Georgia legislature expelled him from elected office because he opposed the draft and the war. The same racist politicians Bond fought at home were busy drafting young black and brown men to die in Vietnam. These officials were not only old-style southern segregationists like Senators James Eastland and John Stennis of Mississippi, but liberal Democrats like Robert McNamara, secretary of defense under Presidents Kennedy and Johnson. In those days McNamara announced his Project 100,000 to induct thousands of young men into the military from the inner cities as part of Johnson's Great Society. These youngsters, illiterate and unemployed, were not even qualified for the military draft until McNamara implemented his "liberal" solution. The Pentagon drafted thousands who failed to meet the standards on the Armed Forces Qualifications Test. McNamara explained this by saying, "The poor of America have not had the opportunity to earn their fair share of the wealth of this nation's abundance, but they can be given an opportunity to serve in their country's defense and they can be given an opportunity to return to civilian life with skills and aptitudes which, for them, and their families, will reverse the downward spiral of human decay."

According to Jorge Mariscal's definitive *Aztlan and Viet Nam: Chicano and Chicana Experiences of the War,* more than half the American soldiers killed in Vietnam were African American, Puerto Rican, Mexican American, Native American, or Asian American; they were sent to early graves instead of the jobs and training programs they were promised. In 1967 a presidential commission found that a "disproportionate" number of soldiers—20.4 percent—killed in action the previous year were African American. At the time no figures were kept for Mexican Americans, but their percentage among those dying on the front lines was similar. Puerto Ricans were listed as fourth in Vietnam combat deaths while their island was twenty-sixth in population ranking in the United States.

That's why Julian Bond wrote his comic book history at the height of the civil rights movement, because he and SNCC, his publisher, believed every person had a right to debate, decide, and vote on the policies affecting their lives. The slogan "Let the people decide," emblazoned on a 1965 SDS button, was unsettling to those in power, especially when it was being demanded everywhere, from the Edmund Pettus Bridge in Selma, Alabama, to the Induction Center in Oakland, California. John Lewis, then the chairman of SNCC and now an honored member of Congress, remarked: "I don't see how President Johnson can send troops to Vietnam and can't send troops to Selma, Alabama."

The peace movement spread from the early days of the student civil rights movement. In 1966 Muhammad Ali, boxing's heavyweight champion, refusing the draft and preparing for prison, sent this message to the world: "My conscience won't let me go shoot my brother, or some darker people, or some poor hungry people in the mud for big powerful America. And shoot them for what? They never called me nigger, they never lynched me, they didn't put no dogs on me, they didn't rob me of my nationality, rape and kill my mother and father. Shoot them for what? How can I shoot them poor people, poor little black people, babies, children, and women? Just take me to jail."

SNCC leader Bob Moses made this observation on seeing a photo of a Vietnamese child: "He was a little colored boy standing against a wire fence with a big huge white Marine with a gun in his back . . . but what I knew was that the people in this country saw a communist rebel. And that we travel in different realities. and that the problem in working for peace in Vietnam is how to change the isolated sense of reality this country has."

At the first national protest against the Vietnam War, organized by Students for a Democratic Society in April 1965, SDS president Paul Potter issued these memorable words: "The real lever for change in America is a domestic social movement." Triggered by a new consciousness, the Vietnam War was linked to the same problems we faced at home: racism, discrimination, poverty, disenfranchised and voteless sharecroppers from the Mississippi to the Mekong Delta. We all hoped students, liberals, and rank-and-file Democrats would awaken, as they eventually did, but the outcome of the

American war would be decided in large part by people of color from America's inner cities whose children were drafted into a war they didn't see as in their interest.

Ghetto after ghetto burned in uprisings that began as the war escalated. The immediate causes were police violence, racial discrimination, and lack of jobs, but it looked like, felt like, and was like Vietnam, a kind of internal colonialism mirroring the invasion and occupation in Saigon. A system of massive and secret surveillance, suppression, and occupation would be imposed in America while Vietnamese dissidents were subjected to the harsher version of the same "pacification." The space for peaceful political reform seemed to be shrinking by the day.

On February 8, 1968, three black student leaders demanding the desegregation of a campus bowling alley at South Carolina State University at Orangeburg were killed by state troopers. Among their comrades and fellow "radicals" were Jim Clyburn, who would one day rise to third in rank among Democrats in the House of Representatives, and Cleveland Sellers, who would become the longtime chairman of black studies at the university.

The grievous losses in 1968 continued, as previously noted, with the deaths of Martin Luther King and Robert Kennedy. Malcolm X, the leading voice from the streets condemning racism and colonialism as well as renouncing a narrow black nationalism, had been gunned down three years before, in February 1965, a victim of internecine warfare within the Nation of Islam. The Black Panther Party emerged on the Oakland streets in 1966, and in the following year there was civil disobedience involving thousands at Oakland's Induction Center during what organizers called "Stop the Draft Week." Bombings and arson by students, a mirror of the black uprisings, began to rise in 1968. Sometimes the struggles were directly linked. For example, in August 1968, mostly black troops from the First Armored Division called an all-night protest against orders to move into Chicago with live ammunition to quell the demonstrations at the Democratic National Convention. Forty-three of them were court-martialed at Fort Hood.

The 1968 trial of Dr. Benjamin Spock, the Reverend William Sloan Coffin, Michael Ferber, Mitchell Goodman, and Marcus Raskin was a sign of profound changes in the movement and the country. Dr. Spock was the most popular pediatrician in America, his advice listened to by millions. Reverend Coffin was chaplain at the Yale Divinity School and a former CIA official. Raskin, thirty-four, was the director of the Washington-based Institute of Policy Studies, which had roots in Kennedy's New Frontier. Harvard graduate student Ferber was on a path to research and writing, and Goodman would become an author, too. They all faced five-year sentences on a charge of conspiracy to counsel, aid, and abet violations of the Selective Service Act. Their prosecutor was Ramsey Clark, attorney general, who himself in later years would demonstrate against the war and defend civil disobedience. The five were carrying out the Call to Resist Illegitimate Authority, a manifesto signed by 327 people on September 27, 1967.

The so-called Chicago Conspiracy Trial, which occurred

in the fall of 1969, was more militant and inspiring, especially to young people, and deeply polarizing as well. Unlike
the Spock trial, it included a far more political and legal di-
mension that aimed at winning "in the court of public opinion" and a well-argued appeal in federal appellate courts. The
mass rallies, protests, and extensive coverage made it a political event occurring nightly on the news. Witnesses for our defense were drawn from the broadened ranks of dissent, including Ramsey Clark, the attorney general of the United States,
against whom the government used every tactic possible to
exclude him from testifying on our behalf in the open courtroom. It was surreal to watch federal prosecutors blocking the
former attorney general from appearing in a federal chamber.
Black Panther Bobby Seale was chained and gagged for asserting his constitutional right to speak in court and defend
himself, a right based in post–Civil War laws. It was a chilling
reminder of chain gangs. The U.S. Seventh Circuit Court of
Appeals rejected the judge and our prosecutors for prejudicial
misconduct. The jury itself had been evenly divided between
findings of guilt and innocence. As for public opinion, sympathy among young people, African Americans, and liberals
ran high, leaving a polarization similar to 2016.

Defenders of the Vietnam War and law and order will
likely always object to such tactics as stealing FBI or other
government files. They will consider absconding with or pour-
ing blood on draft board files as more serious infractions than
"nonviolent acts." Some proponents of nonviolence and radicals who chose jail over the underground objected, too. Those
objections must be balanced, however, by considering the

relative scale of the disobedience and the larger context of official law breaking.

On May 17, 1968, for example, nine devout Catholics led by two priests, Fathers Daniel and Philip Berrigan, stole and burned hundreds of draft records in an effort to spare Americans from deployment to Vietnam. When the brothers were tried that September, they led the courtroom in the Lord's Prayer. A few months later they spilled blood on the files of Dow Chemical, makers of napalm. In the first eight months of the following year, U.S. officials reported 271 "anti-draft occurrences," inflating the Berrigan "threat" to the status of an obstruction to the smooth operation of the war machine. All nine were found guilty in October 1968 of taking U.S. property, destroying files, and interfering with the 1967 Selective Service Act. Sentenced to eighteen years in prison, four of them chose to go underground, including Philip Berrigan. His brother, Daniel, was arrested on August 11, 1970. Another defendant, Mary Moylan, a registered nurse, was harbored by the proliferating underground in America until 1979, when she gave herself up and served two years in jail. Compared to defoliation, napalming, or throwing prisoners into so-called tiger cages on Con Son Island in Vietnam, the actions of these pacifist priests were nonviolent by any reasonable measure. Their actions elicited widespread sympathy among many ordinary Americans wrestling with growing doubt over the war.

In Los Angeles in August 1969, a massive Chicano Moratorium grew out of the earlier student, labor, and civil rights struggles. The moratorium was the largest Chicano outpouring of antiwar sentiment in history. Four were shot and killed that day, including *Los Angeles Times* writer Ruben Salazar, all by county sheriffs. Salazar, a frequent critic of police brutality and racism, died when a tear gas canister blew through his skull while he sat inside a restaurant to avoid the gas. The recovered notes for his next day's column included this: "Chicano Moratorium. Ya Basta!" ("Enough already!")

On March 8, 1971, eight more activists, inspired partly by the Berrigans, shocked the surveillance state by breaking into the Media, Pennsylvania, FBI office and pilfering thousands of files. Their leader was a well-respected antiwar activist, Professor William Davidow of Haverford College. One of those thousands of secret documents bore the mysterious tag COINTELPRO. We would soon learn that this referred to a secret program created by J. Edgar Hoover, the bureau's longtime director, to "expose, disrupt and otherwise neutralize" black and New Left leaders. Hoover stressed neutralizing, rather than containing, us and ordered that "no opportunity should be missed to capitalize upon organizational and personal conflicts of their leadership." Most frightening was Hoover's directive of March 4, 1968, warning that the "rise of a black messiah" must be prevented at all costs. Dr. Martin Luther King was murdered one month later, and Stokely Carmichael, the young, charismatic, and outspoken champion of Black Power, was forced to flee into exile in Africa eight months afterward. The media burglary lifted the curtain on the pervasive and previously secret government spying on thousands of law-abiding Americans.

The eight Media war resisters were never caught by the FBI, choosing instead to stay silent and go about their lives, not telling their stories until decades later when they decided to come clean to Betty Medsger, the original *Washington Post* reporter to whom they had leaked some of the documents. Her 2014 book, *The Burglary: The Discovery of J. Edgar Hoover's Secret FBI*, told the whole remarkable tale. In the same period, two RAND Corporation researchers, Daniel Ellsberg and Anthony Russo, were immersed in deep discussion over what should be done with a forty-two-volume classified study of the origins of the Vietnam War that had been commissioned in 1967 by Secretary of Defense Robert McNamara. The story of the Pentagon Papers disclosures and subsequent Ellsberg-Russo trial were the final episodes leading to Richard Nixon's exposure and impeachment, disgrace and downfall.

The Spock, Catonsville (the trials of the Berrigan brothers), Media, and Pentagon Papers dramas underlined a profound development in the peace movement, toward a kind of disobedience aimed at public disclosure in the media, taking the risk of trial and imprisonment in each case, and seeking ultimate vindication from outraged public opinion. Just as Dr. King tried to break down the walls of segregation, each of these bold actions cut open the walls of secrecy that had closed in on us for a decade. They revealed new secrets from the 1968–71 years, which had common roots going back to the first moments of the Vietnam War and the cover-up of the August 1964 Tonkin Gulf "incident." The Pentagon Papers case was a more serious threat to the surveillance state than any previous one. Defendants Daniel Ellsberg and Anthony Russo had been members of the security apparatus themselves. Their betrayal of their elite status and class could not be countenanced. The wrath of their minders knew no bounds. Men like Kissinger, who had once trusted the Harvard-educated Ellsberg and sought his counsel, felt personally affronted. Ellsberg's defection from the Higher Circles could not be tolerated. Besides indicting Ellsberg and Russo, the Nixon administration sought also to muzzle the mainstream media by seeking temporary restraining orders against the *New York Times* and the *Washington Post*. Continued release of the documents, according to the government, would cause "immediate and irreparable harm to national security," and so the administration sought a court injunction to stop further publication. In another indication of the growing divide within the power elite, the Supreme Court rejected the government's appeal in a 6-3 decision. From then on the state would implode from its own internal contradictions.

Leonard Boudin, an experienced lawyer from a left-wing background, led Ellsberg's defense. Previously, Boudin had defended Dr. Benjamin Spock, Father Philip Berrigan, the Reverend William Sloan Coffin, and Julian Bond. Counsel for Tony Russo was Leonard Weinglass, our trusted lawyer from the Chicago Conspiracy Trial and a former military lawyer. Other attorneys on the Pentagon Papers defense were Dolores "Dede" Donovan, who had defended U.S. soldiers being prosecuted in Saigon, and the Harrisburg defendants, consisting of Philip Berrigan, Sister Elizabeth McAlister, Rev. Neil McLaughlin, Rev. Joseph Wenderoth, Eqbal Ahmad, Anthony Scoblick, and Mary Cain Scoblick. Other defense attorneys included Mark Rosenbaum, Peter Young, and Carol

Sobel, all of whom went on to long careers at the American Civil Liberties Union, the National Lawyers Guild, or other progressive legal centers. The defense team itself had the characteristics of the peace movement's new activism. Not only was it sophisticated in a legal sense, but intense internal discussions had led to a rich compromise between its legal and political dimensions.

The Nixon administration based its thinking on the McCarthy-era prosecutions of alleged Communists, which featured massive media scares about secret Communists working in Hollywood writing screenplays designed to brainwash unsuspecting Americans, with gossip columnist Hedda Hopper and actors John Wayne and Ronald Reagan among the star witnesses for the government. Nixon, who had made his reputation as a scourge of the Left in the era of the Red Scare, assumed Ellsberg could be indicted as though he were the second coming of Alger Hiss. But a new anti-McCarthy sensibility had matured since the fear-ridden fifties and the stalemated Korean War. In this new climate it was impossible to reduce the New Left to a conspiracy pulling the strings via clandestine Communist agents in thrall to a foreign power. Ellsberg, after all, was an anti-Communist, as was Russo.

Key researchers for the defense also came from antiwar movement backgrounds. Sam Hurst was a student body president and activist from the University of Southern California. Paul Ryder arrived in Los Angeles from Princeton in June 1972. "While a student I went to every demonstration I could find, and was jailed three times," he remembered. When he came to Los Angeles, Ryder received his first exposure to the differences on the defense team during an evening meeting attended by the defendants, lawyers, and staff. It started with Morton Halperin, a former aide to Kissinger who had turned against the war. Halperin was one of the defense team's principal strategic architects. Ryder recalled Halperin "laying out the plan as though it was all settled and there was nothing left to do but hand out work assignments. It was entirely legalistic, about technicalities of classification, whose property the Papers were, and so on." Ryder and Hurst, the student activists, took the risk of speaking up for a more political path, supported by Weinglass and, later, by Boudin. At the end of a somewhat tortured discussion, a synthesis of political and legal strategies was forged and agreed upon by all, including Halperin.

Stanley Sheinbaum and his wife, Betty, a daughter of the famous Warner Bros. family in Hollywood, headed the overall defense team. When we first met in 1967, Stanley was a former consultant to the CIA's Michigan State University "agrarian reform" program in South Vietnam. He was also a close friend of Robert Scheer, who in 1965 had written one of the first pamphlets against the war, the groundbreaking *How the United States Got Involved in Vietnam*. Sheinbaum was a trained New Deal economist who was attracted briefly by Ngo Dinh Diem's fantasies of Westernizing Vietnam's vast countryside. When he learned that Michigan State University's program in Vietnam had secret links to the CIA, he was appalled. He told the story to Scheer, then the editor of *Ramparts*, the political and literary magazine of the New Left movement. The magazine blew the whistle on the program in an explosive 1966 cover story that was quickly picked up by the national press. Vietnam politicized Sheinbaum, who ran unsuccessfully that year as a peace candidate in the Democratic primary for the Santa Barbara congressional seat. Two years later, he served as a McCarthy delegate to the 1968 Democratic National Convention and again ran for Congress, losing in the general election. Now he was championing Ellsberg's defense.

Because of the peace movement, Daniel Ellsberg also began to change. He still tears up when recalling young men he witnessed, pacifist resisters like Randy Kehler, choosing prison terms for their beliefs. Tony Russo, for his part, deepened his affinity with the peace movement by the many personal interviews he had conducted for RAND with National Liberation Front detainees. Russo later published a sympathetic portrayal of them and their motivations for his higher-ups and would ultimately evolve into a combination of radical and countercultural Yippie. A sweet man, he suffered, I believe, from undiagnosed chronic post-traumatic stress disorder.

We created the Indochina Information Project to aid the defense team and a range of young activists—Richard and Jill Rodewald, Marin Marcus, Paul Moscowitz, Susan Edelstein, and Bob Gottlieb among them—took responsibility for writing popular summaries and abridgements of the voluminous Pentagon Papers. These digests were distributed in the tens of thousands at public events in 1972 and 1973. Similar crews intent on educating the public as to the Papers' significance included Terry Provance, Bruce Gilbert, and Holly Near. It was an early launching of the "popular education" approach then rapidly expanding among radical political movements around the world.

Witnesses for the defense called to testify at the trial showed the same diversity, ranging from former top Kennedy administration officials—they included, for example, McGeorge Bundy, former national security advisor, John Kenneth Galbraith, former ambassador to India, Arthur Schlesinger Jr., special assistant to the president, and Ted Sorenson, White House counsel—as well as a cross-section of significant activist witnesses like Howard Zinn, Noam Chomsky, Richard Falk, Don Luce, and former Democratic senator Ernest Gruening of Alaska, whose Senate career was ended by his courageous and lonely vote against the Gulf of Tonkin Resolution. I testified as an expert witness about the four Pentagon Papers volumes on negotiations.

All this chronology is to credit the vast webs of peace movement activism that sustained the trial to its end, when federal judge William Byrne, under a storm of public questioning after a *Washington Post* article revealed that President Nixon and his aide John Ehrlichman had secretly offered Byrne the post of FBI director *while the trial was proceeding.* Finally we would learn in red-hot snippets that the White House had assembled its own secret so-called Plumbers Unit, which had committed a series of crimes and black-bag operations, including burglarizing Ellsberg's psychiatrist's Beverly Hills office, presumably in order to gather personal information to be used to blacken Ellsberg's reputation. Nixon reluctantly asked for and received resignations from Ehrlichman and his chief of staff, H. R. Haldeman, thus breaking up his inner circle of henchmen. As disclosures of administration skull-duggery mounted, including the mysteriously missing wiretap records, our defense team started making repeated motions for an evidentiary hearing.

Years later it would be revealed that Nixon, Haldeman, and Ehrlichman had the following exchange on February 7, 1973:

> EHRLICHMAN: The Pentagon Papers trial will be over I would guess in another ten days, two weeks, something like that. It may go longer than that, but I don't think much longer.
> PRESIDENT: They're not going to convict anybody?
> EHRLICHMAN: I doubt it. I would be very surprised.
> HALDEMAN: You never thought they would.
> EHRLICHMAN: I never thought they would, no.

Imagine the blindness of these two advisors at the top of the Nixon White House chain of command! They never expected Ellsberg to be found guilty. Apparently blind loyalty had overtaken their duty to advise the president. Those in the driver's seat had the presidency going off the road.

Haldeman and Ehrlichman left the inner sanctum of power for the federal penitentiary, where they spent eighteen months for perjury, obstruction of justice, and conspiracy. This turn of events was shocking; those who had spent years trying to imprison radical dissenters were now imprisoned themselves. Thirty-eight federal officials besides Haldeman and Ehrlichman went to jail, including the attorney general,

John Mitchell, White House counsel John Dean, special counsel to the president Charles Colson, former CIA officer and security coordinator of the Committee to Re-elect the President James McCord, and the president's Special Investigations Unit officials E. Howard Hunt and Gordon Liddy.

As for Ellsberg, whom Henry Kissinger had once branded "the most dangerous man in America," his conscience and his activism never rested. He would go on to protest nuclear weapons, among other causes, and was arrested in countless demonstrations. Asked by CNN in 2011 how many times he'd been arrested, Ellsberg offhandedly (and without exaggeration) replied, "Oh, about eighty." Ellsberg has campaigned passionately for the new generation of whistleblowers succeeding him: Julian Assange, Chelsea Manning, and Edward Snowden.

Through these trials and various tribulations, we demonstrated that our country's most powerful elites had been driven to give up their former Cold War assumptions by a state and constitutional crisis between the newly named "doves" and "hawks." And we showed that these internal cleavages would not have happened at all without the decisive factor of the most powerful peace and justice movement in American history.

The third strand of the deep antiwar movement was a widespread dissent by the troops themselves, sometimes bordering on mutiny. As the war ground on, the Pentagon found it nearly impossible to raise the morale of its own troops and conscript sufficient numbers of committed soldiers.

When I was growing up, my favorite novel was *From Here to Eternity* by James Jones, the classic 1951 story of the "grunts" subordinated below the officer corps on every base. My father had been hazed or punished by officers above him while serving in San Diego. As a four-year-old, I watched him sitting, humiliated, half naked, on a wooden rail just below the ceiling in the barracks. *From Here to Eternity* captured the absurdity of such abuse of authority long before Joseph Heller's *Catch-22* (1961) or Kurt Vonnegut's *Slaughterhouse Five* (1969).

The underlying dilemma for the U.S. military was how to build and sustain a killing machine out of conscripts from a divided civilian society in which there was growing dissent and urban rebellion. Despite heavy Pentagon discipline, dissent had begun to rise in the armed forces by the mid-sixties just as it had previously on campuses and in ghettos. By the seventies, dissent within the U.S. military had become so widespread that it sharply cut the capacity of the armed forces to wage war. After 1970, the military faced a predicament that resembled DuBois's description of slaves seeking to escape their overseers by walking away from plantations.

One of the great myths about Vietnam concerns an un-bridgeable "divide" between the peace movement and the troops. Indeed, there were class and ideological differences, but everyone came from the same generation, watched the same television news, and began to question the official propaganda against perceptions on the ground. Everyone was equally lied to. Open dissent in the military came early. For example, Special Forces sergeant Donald Duncan, who had served in the Green Berets in 1964 in Vietnam, participat-

ing in intelligence and "hunter-killer" teams, had spoken
out against the war at the May 1965 Berkeley teach-in. Nine
months later, he was on the cover of the February 1966 issue
of *Ramparts*, having written a riveting account of his service
titled "The Whole Thing Was a Lie." That same year three soldiers at Fort Hood—James Johnson, Paul Mora, and David
Samas—publicly announced their decision to refuse orders to
go to Vietnam, and Dr. Howard Levy refused to train Green
Beret medics. By April 1967, the Vietnam Veterans Against
the War (VVAW) declared themselves by unfurling a banner
at the giant protest march in New York City. Then, on the
Fourth of July, three hundred veterans held a peace rally at Independence Hall in Philadelphia. As in the movement to support civil rights in the South, peace activists began that year
to establish GI coffeehouses adjacent to U.S. military bases
as centers for dissent, dialogue, and community building.
Fred Gardner, a member of SDS, was the first to open such a
coffeehouse, known as UFO, near Fort Jackson in Columbia,
South Carolina. In the tradition of community organizing,
he encouraged soldiers to read and discuss the newspapers
and form the earliest of "rap groups" to freely consider their
options. Underground GI newspapers began appearing the
same year—they would eventually number in the hundreds.
Jane Fonda, derided in conservative histories as an "enemy"
of our troops, began her work in the peace movement with
Free the Army (FTA) rallies near U.S. military bases world-
wide, attended by thousands of cheering troops. Clandestine
networks were built to protect deserters or ferry them safely
to Sweden or Canada.

The VVAW would lead a historic protest on Memorial Day

weekend in 1975, with 485 arrested at the old Revolutionary War battleground of Concord, Massachusetts. Hundreds encamped in Washington, DC, and many threw their medals over the Capitol fence. Among them was John Kerry, who challenged the U.S. Senate Foreign Relations Committee with the famous and unanswerable question, "How do you ask a man to be the last man to die for a mistake?" There were more than thirty events classified as "riots" on military bases from 1965 to 1970, from Fort Hood, Texas, and the Presidio in San Francisco to Long Binh and Binh Duc in South Vietnam, as detailed by James Lewes in his excellent *Protest and Survive: Underground GI Newspapers During the Vietnam War*. And that was before the war turned ugly during the years 1971–75.

The statistics tell the story: between 1968 and 1975, ninety-three thousand desertions were reported, triple the scale during the Korean War. Incidents of fragging increased rapidly after 1970. By official estimates there were up to 1,000 attempted fraggings from 1970 to 1972, and 368 courts-martial brought. There were 1.5 million AWOL "incidents," 550,000 desertion "incidents," and an estimated 10,000 soldiers who had gone underground. As for those facing the draft, there were 3,250 who went to prison, 5,500 who received suspended sentences or probation, 197,750 whose cases were dropped, and 171,700 conscientious objectors. More than 500,000 received dishonorable discharges, 164,000 faced courts-martial, and 34,000 were placed in military brigs, according to figures compiled by historians Lawrence Baskir and William Strauss. David Cortright corroborates these astonishing numbers in his book *Soldiers in Revolt*.

Soldiers were withdrawing from the war just as slaves had withdrawn from the grip of the Confederacy, by means small and large, direct and indirect. A January 1970 article by U.S. Navy commander George L. Jackson in the *Naval War College Review* warned that "Negro civil rights action has introduced definite constraints on the military capability of the United States. . . . The factor of morale is extremely important, and a low morale on the part of Negro personnel lessens their effectiveness and that of the forces to which they are assigned." Jackson noted how many troops were deployed "to quell civil disturbances," which diverted them from their overseas mission. During fiscal year 1968 alone, he reported, 104,665 National Guardsmen were used to suppress civil disorders from Washington, DC, to the Madison campus of the University of Wisconsin, "the first case in which Guardsmen were used to restore order on campus." The Detroit "disturbance" alone took 5,547 active army personnel and 10,399 active-duty guardsmen to control.

Marine Corps historian Robert Heinl concluded in a June 1971 article in the *Armed Forces Journal*, "Our army that now remains in Vietnam is in a state approaching collapse, with individual units avoiding or having refused combat, murdering their officers and NCOs, drug-ridden and dispirited where not near mutinous." Heinl compared the army's tribulations to the French army's Nivelle mutinies in 1917 and the disintegration of the czar's armies in Russia in the same year.

Without reliable ground troops, the only military options left to the United States were an escalating air war and the deployment of an ineffective Saigon army. Saigon's military was similar in its corruption to the later Afghan and Iraqi armies, or the earlier Cuban Bay of Pigs invaders, simply unable to match its revolutionary nationalist adversaries. The policy lesson for the United States should have been to avoid any involvement in sectarian-religious wars on the side of traditional colonial clients. The primary interest group lobbying for the Vietnam War was the Catholic Church, which protected a small population of Vietnamese Catholics who were colonized by the French. In addition, U.S. Special Forces recruited a Montagnard tribal minority to fight on the American side. It was folly from the first to believe that the United States could win by rallying Catholics and Montagnards to convert a 90 percent Buddhist country fresh from a triumph over the French. The end of the military draft in 1973—a great victory for the peace movement—was a sign that the Establishment feared the specter of an American civilian army, one of our country's great democratic traditions. Ending the draft meant ending a reliance on soldiers drawn from the rainbow citizenry of our diverse civic society. But the option of ending unpopular, unaffordable wars like Vietnam was out of the question for our stubborn elites. In place of a diverse, multiracial, and often unruly civilian army came the shift to what was hoped would be a more "professional" and reliable force made up of volunteers.

An early exposition of the "necessity" of dirty wars was contained in the 1960 novel *The Centurions* by Jean Larteguy, which extolled the professional warrior class of ancient Rome. *The Centurions* became a favorite work of later generals like David Petraeus, and neoconservative hawks like Robert M. Kaplan, who wrote the introduction to the 2015 reissue. It may be of more than passing interest to know that Petraeus's father-in-law, William Knowlton, was involved in the notorious Vietnam Phoenix Program, known formally as Civil Operations and Revolutionary Development Support (CORDS), which implemented the "strategic hamlets" program — eerily reminiscent of the model of controlling Native Americans on military reservations. Fred Kaplan, in his book *The Insurgents*, described Petraeus as having "devoured" *The Centurions* as "one of his favorite books, period," even going so far as to model his battalion's uniforms after a French officer in the novel. *The Centurions* sympathetically portrayed French colonial officers who had contempt for civilians back on the home front who had little tolerance for or understanding of the need for repugnant measures perceived as necessary in wartime. Torture was rationalized, according to one of the novel's characters, because the Vietnamese enemy would "go to any lengths . . . beyond the conventional notion of good and evil." As a reaction to such beliefs the French antiwar movement rose as a prelude to the later American one.

Concern over the reliability of a civilian army was accompanied by equal worries about the trustworthiness of the democratically elected Congress and the independent mass media. The American failure in Vietnam led directly to an increased reliance on a Big Brother–style surveillance state and secret wars using mercenary troops in remote locations. The threat to democracy signified by Watergate, after a brief democratic thaw, accelerated again during the Central American wars and the Iran-Contra scandal, and over time morphed into today's "full-spectrum" military strategy emphasizing Special Operations, drone attacks, cyber-warfare, and a doctrine of "information war" aimed at manipulating public opinion. When the third Iraq War began in 2014, the 1973 War Powers Act, the single greatest legislative achievement of the Vietnam protest era, was in shreds. When President Obama asked Congress to "rein him in," Congress instead seemed ready to hand all war-making powers back to the secret units of the executive branch.

Today's escalation of secret wars and surveillance originated in the Vietnam era when the government and military became fearful of relying on public opinion or a free press— that is, on democracy itself. Voters became objects of official suspicion, and thus democracy was placed in their emergency care. From the start "national security" experts dominated the media portrayal of the Iraq War with a vested interest in the war itself. The media experts embedded in the television coverage included Lieutenant General Gregory Newbold, director of operations for the Joint Chiefs of Staff; General Charles Horner, air commander of Desert Shield and Desert Storm; Christopher Meyer, British ambassador; and General Buck Kernan, commander in chief, Special Forces Command. NBC hired General Barry McCaffery, then chief of the U.S. Southern Command; CNN, for its part, paid General Wesley Clark, former NATO commander; PBS featured John Warden, architect of the air force's Gulf War operations. And so the list ran on, with every television network hiring military and intelligence experts with interests in the very war they were explaining to the American people and assembled press corps. One could understand how the military mind-set might impede clear and critical thinking. What seemed harder to parse was how the mainstream media had abandoned its ostensible commitment to truth telling and succumbed to war fever on matters of national security, spending huge sums of money to buy "expert" opinions during what was obviously a Pentagon-orchestrated public-relations offensive. At a critical moment, even the august *New York Times* permitted Judith Miller, one of its star reporters, to retail bogus stories about Saddam Hussein's alleged weapons of mass destruction. She wasn't the only one to be used as a cat's-paw by the war party within the White House. False intelligence information found its way into General Colin Powell's United Nations speech supporting the invasion of Iraq, a speech he later regretted. Miller was ultimately purged from the newspaper of record and replaced by a new generation of more independent-minded journalists who answered to a chastened bevy of newly appointed top editors.

Exceptionally, I was interviewed by ABC newsman Ted Koppel along with Ohio representative Dennis Kucinich as the war began. Koppel observed that while those of us who opposed U.S. intervention couldn't end the Iraq War, we certainly could "complicate its prosecution." You would have to search far and wide, however, to discover any media use of expert opinion from voices grounded in the anti–Vietnam War debates of the past. Occasionally, the media might report on the numbers at a protest march or show a Code Pink placard, but serious voices for peace were blacked out of the debate. In fact, when critical voices eventually appeared late in the war, they were usually deemed acceptable only because of their former status in the military or CIA. Anyone jailed in any Vietnam-era protests was effectively disqualified from speaking intelligently about their cause. Of course, if government officials were being fired, resigning in disgrace, or hauled off to jail, that would be newsworthy.

The cancerous course taken by the surveillance state over the past fifty years has its origins in the battles over Vietnam. We would do well to remember them.

By the mid-1970s, the issue of unconstitutional domestic spying against civil rights activists and antiwar organizers dominated the headlines, with revelations from the Church Committee, Senate and House intelligence hearings led by Senator Frank Church (D-Idaho) and Representative Otis Pike (D-New York). At last it appeared that the toxic consequences of Vietnam would be exposed and fixed. Repression of dissent was foremost of these, with the FBI keeping dossiers on 1 million Americans, according to the 1976 *Final Report of the U.S. Senate Select Committee to Study Governmental Operation.*

Most of us in the peace movement underestimated the machinations and durability of the American surveillance apparatus which, like a giant mushroom, grew at night. But hope for accountability breathed anew when Congress approved the formation of two new congressional oversight committees in 1977, though they lacked the full authority to clean house. There followed decades of new revelations, court cases, and dueling "white paper wars" between contending political factions, until finally the 9/11 terrorist attacks in 2001 led to new levels of surveillance justified by terrorist hunting that still dominate the government today. Senator Diane Feinstein (D-California) even uncovered a plot by the CIA to spy on her own committee's professional staff while it prepared a report on the torture of Guantánamo detainees. An internal report by the CIA inspector general confirmed the Feinstein charges, according to *New York Times* reporters Mark Mazzetti and Carl Hulse.

Before this episode fades into collective memory, it must be seen as a case study of power for a new generation of activists, journalists, and historians. The permanent pattern of scandal, exposé, reform, and counterreform is this: the escalation of secretive and press-managed war inevitably is accompanied by the smothering or diverting of dissent, raising the ultimate stakes between democracy and empire. Token changes are then designed to dull the sharp edges of dissent before it spills over to new conflict and disobedience. Step by step, the system that is first targeted for reform is gradually consumed by its original targets, like moss growing over a stone. In this example, the CIA, the original focus of the Church Committee reforms, evolved malignantly until the roles were reversed and today it stands exposed as spying on its own oversight committee. Thus does the fox stealthily creep back into the henhouse.

Despite its best efforts, though, the system is never all controlling, however "effective" its spying and counterintelligence. The more secrets are divulged, the more revelations appear in the media, the more protests erupt. By the nineties, a series of youth-led uprisings, often with labor support, shocked the elites planning to launch the World Trade Organization. For days at a time, starting in Seattle, the protestors "rocked" the elite celebration of corporate dominance over global finance and trade. Protests spread rapidly to many cities: Washington, Philadelphia, Los Angeles, Davos, Berlin, Genoa, London, Montreal, Melbourne, Berlin, London, Prague, and beyond. The protests were directly aimed at the rise of neoliberalism, whose corporate sponsors sought to roll back labor, environmental, and human rights restrictions on trade and investment in what was hailed by boosters as "the new economy." The resistance owed a debt to the models of direct action inspired by the sit-ins and occupations against the Vietnam War in the sixties.

This "Seattle era" featured police and FBI informants, provocateurs armed with pepper spray and rubber bullets, mass data collection, and photos of thousands of marchers. Those extralegal means, however, would fail to halt the "threat." An identical surveillance format was repeated at every site of the antiglobalization protests. As in Chicago in 1968, where the cycle of repression and rebellion began, initially the FBI fed inflammatory false intelligence to nervous local officials. In 1968 it was feared that black militants would seize Chicago's South Side while the Yippies were dosing Lake Michigan with LSD. The FBI scared local press and officialdom with predictions that "the anarchists are coming" by the tens of thousands. In every case, handfuls of suspected "anarchists" were rounded up, hit with pepper spray, served with indictments, and subjected to preventive detention. In the event, the worst-case scenarios of the police failed to materialize and the protestors were released with heavy fines as traditional order was restored with minor adjustments in policing techniques. The cycle kept repeating.

Then came the terrorist attacks of 9/11, catapulting the pattern to the most lethal and threatening levels. Congress immediately passed the U.S.A. Patriot Act, in which the real threat from Al Qaeda replaced the previous "anarchist" and "Communist" threats in the playbook of surveillance and repression. The decline of one set of enemies was followed by the growth of more extreme ones. Today, Al Qaeda has been replaced by ISIS in the rogues' gallery of jihadists. ISIS is a malignant offshoot similar to the genocidal Khmer Rouge that arose after the 1970 American invasion of Cambodia left the country prostrate and vulnerable. Tens of billions of taxpayer dollars now fund counterintelligence, missiles and bombs, surveillance, and Special Forces for deployment in the Middle East with disturbingly sparse evidence of victory on the battlefield. American public opinion has shifted in favor of war by the West against ISIS. This is even more true in France, where the formerly fascist forces, now assembled as the Front National, are gaining ground. The new climate of fear, combined with the billions spent for counterterrorism, virtually guarantees a steady slide into another American war.

This deadly spiral was not inevitable. If the Church Committee really had checkmated the CIA and FBI in 1977, if the Iraq War had been stopped by revelations that Saddam's "weapons of mass destruction" were a canard concocted by our secret branch of power, if the conflicts in Afghanistan, Iraq, and Syria had been settled by enforceable power-sharing arrangements, if the Libyan state had not been shattered into tribal anarchy, if the Egyptian generals had been restrained from overthrowing an elected government in Cairo, perhaps the grim executioners of ISIS might not have progressed on their calamitous path. Instead, Bernard Lewis and other "Arabists" advised that the path to peace was through division and conquest. As he wrote in *Foreign Affairs* in the fall of 1992, "If the central power is sufficiently weakened, there is no real civil society to hold the polity together, no real sense of common identity . . . the state then disintegrates—as happened in Lebanon—into a chaos of squabbling, feuding, fighting sects, tribes, regions and parties."

Most important in retrospect, if the Vietnam-era peace movement had been recognized for its collective knowledge and expertise, then perhaps Washington would have thought twice before rushing into the cauldron of Mesopotamia. Instead of a politics of hysteria, room might have been found within our increasingly fevered and divided political culture for a respected and mainstream politics of peace. Instead, the United States fired Iraq's army from its prewar payrolls and installed a sectarian Shiite government and military in Baghdad with an affinity toward the Shiite Alawite minority dictatorship in Syria. ISIS, powered by Sunni zealots, filled the vacuum. Historical analogy is always fraught, but it is also a mistake to refuse to heed the lessons that experience teaches. Vietnam had—and still has—much to teach us. Tragically, we refuse to learn.

3

O N APRIL 30, 1970, Nixon launched a surprise invasion of Cambodia in violation of both the Constitution and rising public opposition. It was a vain attempt to pinpoint and destroy the supposed "jungle headquarters" of the Vietnamese armed forces, another of his feverish theories that failed but caused massive blowback. In the previous months, events had begun to spiral out of control:

- One of my closest friends, Richard Flacks, coauthor of the *Port Huron Statement* and professor of sociology at the University of Chicago, was high on the government's subversive lists despite a lifetime of nonviolence devoted to reason. On May 5, 1969, he was attacked in his own office by a masked intruder who slashed his wrists and bludgeoned his skull with a claw hammer. The mystery of why he was assaulted was never solved, nor was his assailant ever identified. Flacks, married and the father of two young sons, went on to teach and lead the sociology department at the University of California at Santa Barbara for the next forty years.

• On May 15, 1969, on the orders of California governor Ronald Reagan, Berkeley police, Alameda County sheriffs, state troopers, and the National Guard ripped up the garden at People's Park in Berkeley, killing one innocent person (James Rector), blinding another (Alan Blanchard), wounding fifty-one civilians with birdshot and buckshot, and indiscriminately spraying the University of California campus with pepper gas from a helicopter, which caused schoolchildren as far away as two miles to sicken and vomit.

• On December 4, 1969, two leaders of the Chicago Black Panthers, Fred Hampton and Mark Clark, were shot and killed in their sleep by a Chicago police death squad using floor maps drawn by an FBI informant.

• On March 6, 1970, three members of the newly formed Weather Underground blew themselves to pieces in the basement of a Greenwich Village townhouse while making bombs intended to be used against officers and their dates at a military dance at Fort Dix. Two survivors—Cathy Wilkerson and Kathy Boudin—fled almost naked through the rubble until shocked pedestrians offered them clothing. They vanished further underground.

• On April 7, 1970, Governor Reagan spoke to the Council of California Growers at Yosemite National Park. In response to a question about campus unrest, he said, "If it takes a bloodbath, let's get it over with. No more appeasement."

Meanwhile, a Free Bobby Seale rally was scheduled for May 1, 1970, on the historic Green at Yale University in New Haven, Connecticut. The Black Panther leader was facing charges of having ordered the torture and murder of a suspected informant within the group. The demonstration was expected to draw upwards of twenty thousand people. The city and the fabled Ivy League institution, with a student body of fifty-five hundred, including Hillary Rodham, then in law school with her soon-to-be husband, Bill Clinton, would come under massive occupation by troops, police, and vast numbers of informants and undercover agents. Windows were shuttered on many businesses. I saw young white people carrying baskets of guns in case the final battle might begin. But against all expectation there was peace at Yale that combustible weekend, thanks in part to skilled troubleshooting by campus officials and the steadiness of the Black Panthers and thousands of student activists, including Hillary, who was wearing a black armband.

Kingman Brewster, Yale's president, had been clashing with Vice President Spiro Agnew, who was later forced to resign on federal corruption charges. Agnew's speechwriter, the well-respected William Safire, later a columnist for the *New York Times*, was crafting Agnew's diatribes and relentlessly attacking Ivy Leaguers as if they were a subspecies. Brewster, who represented the moderate wing of the Establishment, chose to take on the Nixon-Agnew crowd on behalf of his students, faculty, and many more American liberals. On April 24, 1970, he famously said of the impending trial of Seale and other Black Panthers on charges of conspiracy to commit murder: "I am appalled and ashamed that things should have come to such a pass in this country that I am skeptical of the ability of black revolutionaries to achieve a fair trial anywhere in the United States."

The night before the rally, April 30, 1970, a group of us met after midnight at Brewster's home. The atmosphere was one of palpable anxiety and panic. Attending, aside from Brewster and myself, were Cyrus Vance, the Reverend William Sloan Coffin, and Ann Froines and her husband, John, Yale PhD '67, who had been involved in the Chicago Conspiracy Trial. The meeting was agreeable, though tense. New Haven police chief James Ahern played a constructive peacekeeping role, arguing against those who favored use-of-force tactics to put down protestors. A potential confrontation was defused. After the meeting ended, the Froineses and I went over to the Branford College Master's House to brief David Dellinger, Yale '36, a conscientious objector and pacifist who had gone to prison during World War II for his beliefs and who had since become a stalwart advocate for the poor and dispossessed in America. He had helped organize the Mobilization to End the War in Vietnam and was a leader of the first major antiwar demonstration, held in New York City in October 1965. He had been rewarded for his tireless efforts against the Vietnam War by becoming one of our fellow defendants in Chicago.

On May 1, I gave a speech on the New Haven Green in which I read out a student call for a nationwide student strike. The response from the gathered students was immediate, spontaneous—and positive.

Meanwhile, in Ohio that same day a rally was held on the

student commons of Kent State University to protest the invasion of Cambodia. In the evening the usual student partying in Kent bars erupted into a skirmish with police. Jerry M. Lewis, a Kent State sociology professor who witnessed the events and subsequently spent years researching what really happened, noted, "The exact causes of the disturbance are still the subject of debate forty years later, but bonfires were built in the streets of downtown Kent" by students, in response to which police tear-gassed the area to clear it and then closed access.

The next day, Saturday, May 2, Kent mayor LeRoy Satrom officially requested that Ohio governor James Rhodes send the National Guard to Kent. By 10:00 p.m., the wooden ROTC building near the commons had been burned to the ground amid student approval. Controversy continues over who set or fanned the blaze—whether it was a spontaneous act, or premeditated arson carried out by either an organized antiwar group or one of many undercover provocateurs sent to the scene. The targeting of ROTC was not exceptional. During the first ten days of May 1970, ROTC buildings were firebombed at more than thirty other colleges and universities all over the country: Hobart College (Geneva, New York), State University of New York (Buffalo), Washington University (St. Louis, Missouri), Middlebury College (Middlebury, Vermont), University of Kentucky (Lexington), Case Western Reserve University (Cleveland), Tulane (New Orleans), Ohio State University (Columbus), Ohio University (Athens), De Pauw University (Greencastle, Indiana), University of Maryland (College Park), Michigan State University (Lansing), Princeton University (Princeton, New Jersey), Oregon State University (Corvallis), Yale University (New Haven, Connecticut), Rutgers College (New Brunswick, New Jersey), Southern Illinois University (Carbondale), University of San Francisco, University of Michigan (Ann Arbor), University of Missouri (Columbia), State University of New York (Brooklyn), John Carroll University (Cleveland), University of Nevada (Reno), College of Colorado (Colorado Springs), University of Virginia (Charlottesville), University of Wisconsin (Madison), University of California (Berkeley), University of North Carolina (Chapel Hill), University of Idaho (Moscow), City College (New York City), University of California (Davis), and Seton Hall University (Orange, New Jersey).

The Ohio Republican primary for an open U.S. Senate seat was scheduled for Tuesday, May 5. Governor Rhodes was on the ballot, running against Robert Taft III, who favored an "irreversible" withdrawal from Vietnam. Rhodes had an incentive to act tough and perhaps by doing so would command the law-and-order votes. On Sunday, May 3, one thousand National Guardsmen occupied the campus. Governor Rhodes held a press conference denouncing the students as "brownshirts" who would be "eradicated." Confrontations continued into the night.

On Monday, May 4, students gathered in a rally to protest the official ban on protests, despite the university administration having issued twelve hundred leaflets prohibiting rallies as long as the guardsmen patrolled the campus. By noon the commons area was filled with three thousand people. There were an estimated five hundred "core" demonstrators,

about one thousand supporters, and probably upwards of fifteen hundred spectators around the edge of the commons.
Around noon, General Robert Canterbury of the Ohio National Guard ordered his troops to disperse the demonstrators and to lock and load with live ammunition. On the top
of Blanket Hill, twenty-eight of the seventy-plus guardsmen
huddled, then suddenly turned and opened fire—between
sixty-one and sixty-seven shots within thirteen seconds. Four
students were killed, one shot in the back.

Later, the official Scranton Commission appointed by
Nixon to investigate the tragedy concluded that "the indis-
criminate firing of rifles into a crowd of students and the
deaths that followed were unnecessary, unwarranted and in-
excusable." But at that point, students all over the country
began to realize that student lives didn't matter.

A year later, in 1971, James Michener would publish a
best-selling book alleging that SDS had cynically conspired
to manipulate Kent State students into putting themselves in
harm's way, hoping that violence would erupt, to garner sympathy for the cause. As the tragedy unfolded, the group's militants lurked, according to Michener, in a so-called haunted
house near campus, a nearly abandoned home virtually in
shambles. For his spin efforts, he was welcomed to the Nixon
White House. The truth was that SDS was a spent force in
Kent. A later FBI investigation found no evidence to substan-
tiate such suspicions. Indeed, SDS had been banned from the
campus and its few members were fighting the cost of felony
charges that had been brought against them.

But facts didn't matter much in a world of spin, partisan

feuds, and propaganda. The battle over Vietnam—and later its legacy—took place in a contested ideological combat zone with sparring spin doctors everywhere at work. The struggle persisted even decades later. For example, in his 2005 book *13 Seconds,* esteemed author Philip Caputo actually blamed the Kent students themselves for throwing "a collective destructive tantrum" and causing their own deaths.

On May 8, 130,000 antiwar protestors came to Washington, DC, and another 150,000 to San Francisco, to demonstrate against the Cambodia invasion and the killings at Kent State. *New York Times* columnist Max Frankel wrote on May 10 that the domestic upheaval "sent tremors of fear throughout the White House that revolt and repression might be nearer than anyone had dared to imagine."

May Day the next year, 1971, brought a dramatic effort, the brainchild of Rennie Davis, one of the Chicago Conspiracy Trial defendants, to hold a protest that would shut down the government by clogging the streets in Washington, now circled by tanks and armored vehicles. In the end, 12,614 people were rounded up and held in RFK Stadium in Washington and local lockups in Virginia and Maryland. It was the largest mass arrest in U.S. history.

Despite the mounting protests, it turned out that Nixon had nothing to fear—he was elected by a landslide in November 1972. The crimes of Watergate had yet to be exposed. Just days before the November vote, Nixon and Kissinger orchestrated a media blitz beginning on October 26 with the national security advisor's statement that "peace is at hand," a transparent ploy to assure the electorate that a settlement was in the offing and that it would be a mistake to abandon the president at a moment when peace was around the corner. In fact, Nixon and Kissinger were planning for a massive use of force against Hanoi at Christmastime. Nixon's tapes show that he wanted, as he said to Kissinger, to "destroy the goddamned country" with "even the nuclear weapon."

Jane Fonda's much-condemned trip to North Vietnam that year was intended to bring world attention to a threat of bombing the ancient dikes sustaining Vietnam's agricultural economy. She was right. The White House tapes for April 25, 1972, record the following exchange between President Nixon and national security advisor Henry Kissinger:

> PRESIDENT: I still think we ought to take the dikes out now. Will that drown people?
> KISSINGER: About 200,000 people.
> PRESIDENT: No, no, no . . . I'd rather use the nuclear bomb. Have you got that, Henry?
> KISSINGER: That, I think, would just be too much.
> PRESIDENT: The nuclear bomb, does that bother you?
> . . . I just want you to think big, Henry, for Christ sakes.

In a later exchange, Nixon told Kissinger, "The only place where you and I disagree . . . is with regard to the bombing. You're so goddamned concerned about the civilians and I don't give a damn. I don't care." Kissinger replied: "I'm concerned about the civilians because I don't want the world to be mobilized against you as a butcher." Kissinger's estimate of

200,000 deaths from an attack on the dikes exceeded the initial death toll from the U.S. atomic bombing of Hiroshima at the end of World War II, which, according to Howard Zinn's 2010 book *The Bomb*, was 140,000; the immediate toll from the Nagasaki bombing was 70,000.

Our younger generation today should know these were times in twentieth-century America when, in the words of Reinhold Niebuhr, our foremost theologian, writing in the February 8, 1965, issue of *Christianity and Crisis*, "We are making Vietnam into an American colony, ruining an unhappy nation in the process of saving it." It was a time when nuclear strategist Herman Kahn was encouraging us to think about the unthinkable and use nuclear weapons. For today's youth, the unthinkable has become the inconceivable—yet we still exist on the brink of disaster.

The most important lesson of these traumatizing experiences is the paradoxical one that, as I once told my friend Marshall Gans, "Social change happens very, very slowly," and yet change comes suddenly and unexpectedly in the form of the future itself. The movements for civil rights, peace, justice, and women's rights all arose at the extreme margins of society and were ridiculed and harassed by the Machiavellian class until they gained support from the wells of our progressive history, became majority movements, created new norms, and elected national leaders. Even in triumph they were forced to contend with countermovements within our culture, our political system, the corporations, and the military. They faced everything from assassination to co-optation to venal corruption and clashing egos, in an unending cycle.

Thus do movements of reform and radical change rise and fall, and rise again. The alchemy of change isn't a science. It is elusive and unpredictable. What is certain, however, is that the yearning for justice and dignity is inextinguishable, for it defines us as a species seeking to give meaning to our otherwise inchoate lives.

Our redwoods are two thousand years old, grown from the seeds of their ancestors. Over the centuries they become life forms that shelter an ecosystem of many more life forms. They are threatened by storms, lightning, fire, earthquakes, and the savage blades of forest workers and industrial development. And still they survive. They arrive, finally, at their climax phase, an exuberant spurt of multicolored foliage. Social movements follow a similar course, from seeds to saplings to maturity, through storms and failures, until they, too, climax in exuberance, scattering seed again.

The Vietnam peace movement began with the seeds of our ancestors. We continued dispersing the seeds until we grew into a movement of many tendencies, colors, and directions. Like a natural life form, it declined and grew again. But in its climax stage, it had a powerful impact on the American landscape. Beginning with tiny growths at the margins, we learned the process of organizing a mass public opposition to shake off the powers of oligarchy. In the end, we democratized America. It was the only way the war might end. Nixon admitted as much in a July 7, 1969, memo to his aides warning that public support for the war would last only "until about November," which was the time of that year's historic moratorium. On September 10, 1969, Kissinger had already told the president: "The pressure of public opinion [is] on you to resolve the war quickly, and I believe [it will] increase greatly, in the coming months. The plans for student demonstrations in October are well known, and while many Americans will oppose the students' activities, they will also be reminded of their own opposition to the continuation of the war." Those statements are among the most definitive official acknowledgments of the power of a peace movement that the administration had continued to deny. Earlier, according to David Maraniss's book, *They Marched into Sunlight*, the same fears were leading LBJ himself to float the idea of dropping out of the 1968 presidential race as early as 1967.

Beginning in 1968, the sixties generation had burst into uprisings around the world that would never be forgotten. The Vietnam War was central to that global resistance, a burning symbol of generational revolt. Asked by the Johnson administration to scour the youth rebellion for evidence of Soviet or Chinese funding and guidance, the CIA could find no such substantiation in a country-by-country assessment it supplied to White House advisor Walt W. Rostow. (Fully forty years later, German scholars Martin Klimke and Joachim Scharloth published a twenty-six-chapter study of mainly European anti-Vietnam movements that drew the same conclusion.)

How exactly was a sprawling and quarreling peace movement, especially a global one, organized at all? Obviously Lyndon Johnson, Richard Nixon, and their blundering generals played the key role in generating public antagonism to government policy. But there was something new in the air during this post-McCarthy era. The civil rights and global student movements represented a new consciousness outside the either-or confines and categories of the Cold War. The peace movement was a movement against an infernal never-ending war, to be sure, but it also was a movement for the intangible ideal of a better world. It was no accident that Woodstock and the huge moratorium made their surprise appearances at about the same time, the summer and fall of 1969. Everything was discovered to be related. One movement followed another, first by example and then by transference of energy to a new particularity, one impulse toward liberation leading—leaping—to the next. It was an awakening like few others in history, and seemed more self-propelled than dictated, more destined than accidental.

How was youthful passion channeled into effective action? Historians may never know. It all took place fifty years before e-mail, Twitter, or Facebook. Communication in 1964 was via WATS (wide-area telephone service) lines, which allowed a subscriber to make outgoing or incoming calls at a bulk rate. Western Union was a second tool. Conference calls were just being born. Old-fashioned, handwritten letters in a stamped envelope were the standby. The *Port Huron Statement* was mailed in manila envelopes to about sixty-five people on the eve of the June 1962 meeting that would see the founding of Students for a Democratic Society. We used mimeograph machines—remember those?—to crank out our leaflets. In today's world these technologies sound primitive, even prehistoric, but they served as circuits for information drawing thousands to meetings large and small. They enabled a SNCC organizer to alert hundreds of people that a field secretary had gone missing in Mississippi and supply the names of reporters and Justice Department officials to send urgent telegrams to. Instead of today's blizzard of social media, something was in the air itself—an interpersonal connectedness far deeper than bulk communication without soul. All this was somehow generated by a distress signal coming from the obscure country of Vietnam. The Vietnamese believed themselves to be the center, or focal point, of all the world's contradictions. They were not wrong.

What was the movement-building process like in communities? Of thousands of examples, take the case of one of the most seminal, the first Vietnam teach-in of spring 1965. With the draft and initial dispatch of U.S. troops escalating, emotions were stirred on the Ann Arbor campus, where many student activists had been affected by the black student sit-in movement of the previous year. Now the Selective Service was reaching into our lives. If there could be a sit-in to block business as usual under segregation policies affecting us personally, why not a "teach-in" to refute the conformity of our apathetic academia?

Graduate students and faculty launched a series of small meetings at one professor's home, where differences of opinion spilled out immediately. On one side were those who called for a strike. Fearing they could be isolated, dismissed, or expelled, others searched for a less controversial alternative before settling on a middle ground. After hours of agonized meetings, a consensus formed that the university should convert itself into a round-the-clock forum for lectures, discussions, and debate on the subject of the war, which already was disturbing campus life. U.S. Vietnam policy would be researched, discussed, and debated as never before, on the grounds that students had a right to know the rationale for their possible conscription into a war zone. Hawkish professors, State Department officials, and Pentagon spokesmen would be invited to make their case before an audience willing to challenge authority, an audience whose own futures, even lives, were at stake.

Advocates of a faculty strike felt that the proposed teach-in was too passive, a sellout to the administration and U.S. government. No one would be arrested during a teach-in, compared with the harassment and punishments inflicted on lunch-counter sit-in participants. On the more moderate side of the debate, worries grew that the university administrators might not even permit the teach-in on university property. State Republicans and their allies on the Board of Regents demanded that classes be taught as usual, with a threat of consequences for those who questioned the academic status quo.

In the end, what happened was one of the most successful and long-remembered events of the sixties, with thousands of students and their professors forming a single university community to fulfill the mandate of research, questioning, and discussion at the heart of the university's mission. As a result, the nascent antiwar movement was hugely strengthened and seeds were cast, leading to the Senate hearings by Senator William Fulbright the following year. As the teach-in altered the status quo in academia, the Fulbright hearings broke the silence in Washington. And instead of co-optation of the student critics, the outcome was to heighten the stakes in a conflict between activist students, radical intellectuals, and Cold War intellectuals. The organizing principle was not to take the most radical or most purely principled stand but to engage with and listen to the expressed needs of our constituency, the students, for a voice in the decisions affecting their lives.

The first campus political party was aptly named VOICE. Out of apathy and cacophony came the stirrings of a democratic public in place of the suffocating rhythms of mass society. That was the essence of the participatory democracy ideal. The end was also the means to the end. Diversity was respected as a means to greater unity and factionalism frowned upon as an irritating foreign interference in a valuable process of deliberation and action. Inherent in the same process, like it or not, was a radicalizing tendency by which demands were steadily escalated from modest to more militant, issues were broadened from a single focus to an overextended menu, and passions rose accordingly. Often it seemed we were unifying the few against the many, instead of the other way around. Some came to believe that instead of aiming to end the current war, our mission was to end "the seventh war from now," as the saying went. The Vietnam War ended in 1975, and forty years later it appears we are nearing the seventh war from then.

An abiding question was whether the purpose of an organizing campaign was to "radicalize" rank-and-file newcomers or to accomplish the original goal. To radicalize consciousness had an overtone of elitism, echoing Lenin's call for vanguards to export revolutionary thought to workers at a "lower" level of consciousness, who would otherwise be ensnared in the "trap" of reformism, if left to their own devices. The Leninist message meant that activists shouldn't want their original reform proposals adopted at all, except as steps to revolution. In this maximalist view, ending the draft or ending the Vietnam War would never be enough to fundamentally alter the presiding political and economic order, even though lives were saved in the process.

While many on the left grew desperate and felt marginalized at the time, the paradox was that more and more Americans from the center of the political spectrum were persuaded that the unending war was unaffordable and unwinnable. Growing numbers of our fellow citizens became a constituency of conscience, shocked by military calamities like the My Lai massacre or massive media cover-ups or the irreversible defunding of antipoverty programs. They demanded an Earth Day instead of darker nights of war. To everyone's amazement, during the same time as photographs appeared of bleeding Vietnamese villagers in a ditch, Americans glimpsed planet Earth from outer space. A handful of students, led by Senator Gaylord Nelson (D-Wisconsin), mobilized the first Earth Day on April 22, 1970, in a celebration engaging 20 million Americans. What were we doing in Vietnam amid this celebration of our planet?

The most important political change in the seventies was the widening of the peace constituency to create an opening to electoral politics, symbolized by the lowering of the voting age to eighteen, creating a public eager to participate in presidential and congressional peace campaigns. Nixon's Middle

America had softened with age, sickened by war and ashamed of antagonizing their own children. They'd had enough of the Official Line. The opportunity for broader antiwar organizing was opened by Watergate, and by what came to be known as an "inside-outside strategy" of mounting grassroots pressure on politicians in districts and states where the antiwar movement, including returning Vietnam veterans, had done its job of old-fashioned public persuasion. Casting a vote was infinitely easier than resisting a draft notice, and it served the purpose of building a greater public constituency for peace. And so we entered the mainstream, just as many of us tried the decade before, without success, to win support for voting rights and the Mississippi Freedom Democratic Party against the party of war and segregation. In both cases, the results would be lasting but gradual, slow to achieve, and vulnerable to domestic counterattack.

We had to keep public attention on the drama of Vietnam, bringing pressure to bear on candidates and incumbents wherever possible. This was difficult amid the media impression that the war was "winding down," with its implication that our attention belonged on other issues, like the energy crisis. But Nixon was escalating the bombing while he withdrew thousands of American troops, so the horrors of the war kept coming home to render complacency impossible. It was time to go public in more powerful ways.

Jane Fonda, whom I met in 1971 and married in 1973, was a magnetic public personality who had been shaken by Vietnam while living in France and by her involvement with American soldiers on military bases from stateside to the

Pacific. Young servicemen flocked to rallies at bases organized by Jane and her fellow actor Donald Sutherland under the ironic banner of FTA (Free the Army), with its image of fists raised in the air. Everyone understood that the acronym really meant "Fuck the Army," a sentiment shared by disgruntled GIs fed up with a military whose deceptions and callous disregard for the troops under its care were widely disparaged and lampooned. Later, Jane would star with Jon Voight in *Coming Home*, a 1978 movie about a woman whose Marine husband is fighting in Vietnam and who falls in love with another veteran who had suffered a paralyzing combat injury there. The film was inspired by Ron Kovic, a war hero and close friend who was rendered paraplegic for the rest of his life. Both Jane and Voight won Academy Awards for their performances.

At this stage of the faltering antiwar movement, leadership came from advocates of electoral politics within the mainstream, starting above all with the young volunteers who in 1967 wintered in snowy New Hampshire for the quixotic campaign of Minnesota senator Eugene McCarthy.

The war was becoming political. The offices of progressive politicians were cranking into action for the first time. By 1972, the educational road show format evolved into the national Indochina Peace Campaign (IPC) headlined by Jane in more than ninety cities, from synagogues in New Jersey to the Ohio State Fair. Jane was not only charismatic but also a good crowd mobilizer and organizer who easily connected with grassroots folks.

My forty undergraduate students at Immaculate Heart College in Los Angeles, a haven for antiwar Catholics, worked overtime to transform their readings on Vietnam into portable silk-screened poster exhibitions that could be unpacked swiftly to turn an empty room into a graphic environment festooned with images of Vietnamese children, lines of Vietnamese poetry, and chilling quotes from Pentagon officials. Speakers who came to the class included Ron Kovic, whose memoir of his wounding in Vietnam, *Born on the Fourth of July*, would later be turned into a Hollywood movie directed by Oliver Stone and starring Tom Cruise. Others included former POWs like George Smith, a West Virginia postman, who was captured by the National Liberation Front in the late 1960s; young folksingers like Holly Near, Rita Martinson, and Len Chandler; a French activist named Jean-Pierre Debris, who had been captured and tortured by the Saigon government; and a brooding intellectual named Fred Branfman, who single-handedly researched and exposed the U.S. air war over the Plain of Jars in Laos. A USAID worker, Fred had lived, traumatized, among Laotian villagers. Now he lived in Santa Monica with his Vietnamese wife, Thoa, in a space resembling a jungle hideaway, complete with mats and palms. It was an eclectic collective. Kovic often set the tone as he sat in his wheelchair, ending his presentations by saying he'd lost his body but gained his soul and mind. The time was a second dawn for us, a rebirth of the idealism that had originally driven us forward in the early sixties. We argued that the Watergate crisis represented a conflict in the American Establishment brought on by the Indochina War, giving the peace movement its best chance yet to finally end U.S. involvement. We insisted to a doubting audience that this opportunity arose from the

Nixon administration's subverting the American democratic process by breaking laws in pursuit of an unachievable and immoral victory in Indochina.

We believed that our movement had broadened to the mainstream, and that the power elite itself had fallen into warring factions, partly because of pressures from the movement itself. Hillary Rodham, soon to be Clinton, was a McCarthy intern in 1968, witnessing the street confrontations in Chicago. Her future husband, Bill Clinton, was in graduate school in England in 1968, but by 1972 had signed up as George McGovern's campaign organizer in Texas. Those campaigns were the core of the moratorium and reform Democratic politics for the next generation.

In preparing our national antiwar campaign, IPC designed a Vietnam Peace Pledge suiting the mood of the times, calling for the termination of congressional war funding, cutting off aid to Saigon's brutal police and prison systems, and demanding a political settlement through negotiations. The last point was illustrated by a poster depiction of a Vietnamese peasant in a traditional conical hat, demanding, "No More Broken Treaties." It was a time when many Americans, already shaken by Vietnam, were awakening to the trail of wars and betrayals against indigenous peoples on the American frontier. The 1954 Geneva conference, we were learning, was only among the most brazen betrayals against self-determination, overriding the aspirations of millions of Vietnamese people. In addition to arming Saigon forces, the CIA was organizing Vietnam's mountain tribesmen, the Montagnards, to serve as scouts for the United States, as though the operations were little more than a continuation of the U.S. Seventh Cavalry on the western frontier.

Antiwar activists in local coalitions readily carried the pledge draft to the district offices of their congressional representatives, demanding a discussion with elected officials, and kept coming back until a given politician was categorized as "Yes," "No," or "Undecided." (The techniques for keeping updated scorecards on an incumbent politician's stance on controversial issues became known as "bird-dogging." Today, in the age of social media, these techniques can become explosive.) The presentations were designed to reflect the local interests of a particular district, with delegations from the clergy, Mothers for Peace, draft-eligible students, and an increasing stream of returning veterans. Within a few months, at least fifty members of the House and twenty senators were leaning toward endorsing the pledge, a significant minority numerically but also representing which elections mattered. The pledge became a unifying tool for the insurgent grassroots McGovern campaign, which already was drawing together all the strands of the sixties revolt—women, people of color, veterans, reform Democrats, even Yippies like Abbie Hoffman and the Beat poet Allen Ginsberg.

This was the opening phase of a carefully planned political offensive to finally end the war and repudiate the cynical Nixon-Kissinger doctrine of "winding down" the conflict. That strategy became a template for future administrations, as weary and demoralized American troops were dramatically withdrawn while U.S. bombing and deployment of mercenaries and Saigon army units actually escalated. For example, from 1965 to 1968, Johnson dropped 214 tons of bombs in Cambodia. From 1969 to 1973, Nixon dropped 2,756,727 tons of bombs on that country, as reported by Ben Kiernan and Taylor Owen of the Yale University Genocide Studies Program.

IPC's strategic focus was to apply "people power" to the shaky pillars of Nixon's policy in congressional districts. We had concluded that while the Left and the antiwar movement were in sharp decline, there was a striking rise of antiwar public sentiment even in Nixon's "Middle America." By January 1971, the Gallup polling organization found that of respondents with an opinion, 66 percent agreed that the United States had made "a mistake sending troops to Vietnam." That was a base with which we could work.

Nixon was stimulating further withdrawal sentiment by bringing troops and POWs home. People asked why a war should be prolonged if it was winding down. The June 17, 1972, break-in at the Democratic National Committee was an embarrassing criminal act led by former CIA agents and right-wing Cuban exiles. Suspicion of Nixon's dirty tricks escalated with the June 1973 revelation of a White House "enemies list." The pillars were crumbling steadily.

As mainstream public opinion turned against the war, we were increasingly aware that we were no longer isolated radical outsiders. After a decade of exclusion, some movement activists were inclined to reject working within the system, lobbying Congress and supporting candidates. Opportunity was before our eyes, but we were in danger of being bypassed by history. We needed the will and the tools to take advantage of a transition to the legislative and electoral sphere. We none-theless also continued our unorthodox methods: fighting for the release of Saigon's political prisoners, dispatching a dele-gation to unfurl banners against torture at the U.S. embassy in Saigon, where the prisoners were arrested and deported, distributing thousands of wristbands with the names of indi-vidual Vietnamese prisoners, demonstrating against South Vietnam president Nguyen Van Thieu's visit to the San Cle-mente White House, working closely with Ron Kovic and Bobby Mueller of VVAW to broaden the base of the move-ment.

We sought to build sympathetic constituencies in Demo-cratic states, big cities, and college towns. We chose to build an educational and lobbying infrastructure in New York, Mas-sachusetts, Pennsylvania, Ohio, Illinois, Wisconsin, and Cali-fornia, which represented 189 electoral votes, and attempted to reach into Michigan, New Jersey, Oregon, and Washing-ton State. We built on preexisting and experienced veterans of the peace movement, whether the Syracuse Peace Coun-cil, the American Friends Service Committee, led by John McAuliff, draft opponents like Ira Arlook, Berkeley radicals like Jack Nicholl and Carol Kurtz, or experienced coalition builders like Philadelphia's Alex Knopp. We even deployed a Washington, DC, lobbyist to set in motion a district-by-district lobbying effort. He was Larry Levin, a former Bobby Kennedy worker. I met him in his Venice, California, apart-ment, and found him entranced with Irish nationalist ballads and marching songs. Larry came on board and proved a very valuable player in the nation's corridors of power.

Liberalism shared the blame for the war. Vietnam had begun very much as a liberal's war, and that began to change only after the civil rights, women's, and environmental movements rose to challenge the traditional Democratic hierarchy, especially the CIA-directed AFL-CIO, which fumed and plotted against the New Left and the McGovern forces. Institutional realignment happened gradually, and with astonishing vitriol.

The Indochina Peace Campaign did not see itself as an ideological group on the left, nor as a party in the making, not even as a so-called pre-party formation. We didn't compete with other antiwar coalitions. We aimed to create a united front, drawing together many strands of dissent. We also were a catalyst for a new swelling of popular support, overlapping the moratoriums' base. Democrats flocked to our message after many years of Cold War internecine combat. Serious questions arose over the call from Averell Harriman himself, a godfather of the Wise Men, to support the moratorium. Clearly some kind of realignment of the Democratic Party was under way.

The concept of an "inside-outside" strategy was never seen as a contribution to the Sacred Scriptures of the Left. It was based on the knowledge that public opinion was far ahead of the Left's culture of splinter groups. We debated at length, but never resolved how our plans fit into any larger revolutionary aspirations, or whether we fit at all. A vexing question was whether Vietnam was some kind of "mistake," or whether it was somehow systematic, a logical outcome of an imperial strain within the power elites. If the latter, it followed somehow that we had to defeat imperialism on the road to ending the war, an impossible task guaranteed to wear us down. Those debates went on until the war itself ended, and then erupted again during the wars across the Middle East in the early years of the twenty-first century.

This panorama of rising movements and favorable opinion polls was the underpinning of our inside-outside strategy. One had to be seriously out of touch to ignore the possibilities of relatively radical reform, starting with the objective of ending the Vietnam conflict. Starting from the margins, the movement fought its way into the mainstream.

From 1973 to 1975, public pressure on Congress played a decisive role in bringing the war to its end in 1975. The complex nature of power, obscures what really happened at the end. Congress never actually voted to cut off all funding for Indochina, and the Democrats never elected an antiwar candidate to the White House. That's plenty of evidence for those who still believe pressure politics is ineffective and irrelevant to outcomes. On the other hand, what was the prolonged political confrontation leading to Watergate all about? Was it just smoke and mirrors?

One clue can be found in an inner law of power: neither American presidents nor Machiavelli's Prince ever wanted to appear to lose a war or their underlying reputation for sobriety in a realpolitik world. After all, everyone knew that the greater the reputation, the greater the access to allies, votes, and contributions. A fall in reputation attracted termites, rivals, and loss of the fundamentals of holding power.

According to the *Quarterly Congressional Almanac*, in the

decade between the 1964 Tonkin Gulf Resolution and the 1974 Peace Agreement, "Congress cast scores of votes to restrict or terminate the U.S. role in Vietnam, but Congress never was united or successful in its attempts to bring U.S. involvement to an end." And further: "Up to the spring of 1973, Congress gave every president everything he requested regarding Indochina policies and funding," according to the House Democratic Study Group.

By 1970, after the moratoriums, antiwar legislation was first proposed by the Democratic majority leader, Mike Mansfield, Democratic senators Frank Church and George McGovern, and Republican senators John Sherman Cooper and Edward Brooke. This was the first wedge to open debate after the Fulbright hearings. In 1971, two "end the war" amendments, from Representative Mark Hatfield (R-Oregon) and Senator McGovern, were turned down. In that same year, the Senate adopted Mansfield's amendments setting a deadline for troop withdrawals for the first time. A Cooper-Church amendment making military funding contingent on U.S. troop withdrawals was beaten back by a series of close votes in the Senate.

The peace movement noticed with growing interest that the number of antiwar roll call votes jumped from five in 1969 to thirty-five in 1972. The battle was becoming year-round. Despite McGovern's crushing defeat by Nixon, the inside-outside campaign to end the war accelerated from 1972 to 1975. By August 1972 the Senate finally passed an amendment cutting off funding for the war on a tense 49-47 roll call vote. The measure included a four-month timetable for withdrawing troops. In conference committee, the House members opposed the amendment, but the peace movement had won over half the legislative branch of government.

The peace agreement was signed on January 23, 1973, by the United States, North Vietnam, U.S. ally South Vietnam, and the Provisional Revolutionary Government of South Vietnam. The presence of North Vietnamese troops in the South was legitimized in the text along with formal recognition of the National Liberation Front's provisional government and armed forces. The agreement was a demoralizing blow from which Saigon would never recover. At the same time, the agreement left open a face-saving path toward an organized and phased transition to a reunified Vietnam representing the North, South, and so-called third force nationalists and neutralists. In other words, this was a power-sharing transition approved by U.S. negotiators. For Saigon and its diehard backers in Washington, however, it was writing on the wall that the end was at hand.

In May 1973, the House for the first time voted to cut off taxpayer funds for military operations in Cambodia and Laos. Two months later, in July 1973, Congress passed what the *Quarterly* called a "tough war powers measure" that required a forty-eight-hour notice to Congress prior to the executive branch sending U.S. troops into "hostilities abroad," combined with a sixty-day final deadline on a presidential commitment of any such troops. Despite the ambiguities and loopholes, the War Powers Resolution was to become the most important obstacle to executive war ambitions, placing procedural congressional limits on the president's unilateral war-making powers. Among the loopholes in the War Powers Act were the following: (1) there were no sanctions short of impeachment if the president failed to comply with the law; (2) in the phrase "consult with Congress," the word *consult* was undefined, and presidents since have interpreted it to mean mere notification of Congress; (3) a president was able to ignore the law by declaring the use of armed forces to be "humanitarian" rather than "military"; (4) the law established a clock that limited military action to sixty days without need of any authorization for the use of military force or a formal declaration of war. This substantial loophole allowed the president to start military action without starting the clock. Nonetheless, the War Powers Act was a sharp restraint on the imperial presidency, creating space for public protest to be taken into account. A president found in violation of the War Powers Resolution would pay a political price. But every American president since then, including Barack Obama, has threatened to veto the legislation for its implied restraints on the presidency.

Nixon was coiled and ready for another counterattack, even at the expense of peace, if North Vietnam violated the Paris Agreement. Once the remaining twenty-five thousand U.S. troops and all 591 American POWs were returned, Nixon escalated the war against Hanoi at Christmas, saying his bombing campaign would be "massive and brutal in character." (The bombing started on December 18 and ended on December 29, with a thirty-six-hour pause over Christmas.) What "threat" from Hanoi justified the Christmas bombing was never clear, but the American response was completely asymmetrical. The Nixon administration wrongly assumed that Hanoi would "crack quickly."

The lumbering B-52s took off from bases in Guam and

Thailand, their confident crews listening to Henry Mancini's "Baby Elephant Walk" on headphones. The Pentagon had completely underestimated the defenses of Hanoi. The B-52 "elephants" started crashing in the jungle. Vietnamese historians would describe what happened as a Dien Bien Phu in the skies.

On the first two nights, eight B-52s were shot down, sending "shock waves of alarm" through the Nixon administration, according to the military historian Marshall Michel, who had himself flown 321 combat missions over Hanoi. His 2002 book, *The Eleven Days of Christmas*, is a riveting account. The United States dropped fifteen thousand tons of bombs. Two hundred fifty Vietnamese were killed on Kham Thien Street in a largely civilian neighborhood. The old Bach Mai hospital was flattened, killing twenty-five medical staff and burying many patients alive. The toll was an estimated sixteen hundred Vietnamese dead in Hanoi and three hundred in Haiphong.

Over the next eleven days, the Vietnamese shot down fifteen B-52s and badly damaged another five. Twenty-eight U.S. crew members were killed and thirty-four captured on the ground. Never before had a single B-52 been lost in combat, not once in 112,000 missions over seven years since the bombing began in 1965.

During the siege, four American peace leaders flew into Hanoi to bear witness: the singer Joan Baez, Telford Taylor, a retired general who had been involved in the Nuremburg trials, Michael Allen, assistant dean of the Yale Divinity School, and former army lieutenant Barry Romo from Vietnam Veterans Against the War. Baez wrote and recorded an unforgettable lament from a bomb shelter in Hanoi's center, titled "Where Are You Now, My Son?" The twenty-one-minute recording of that Hanoi visit, including the sound of bombs falling and Vietnamese voices, can be heard on You-Tube. It should be included in any postwar memorials or commemoration.

Forty years later, when I visited Hanoi in December 2012, I discovered the musty bomb shelter in its original shape beneath the old colonial Metropole Hotel, now enjoyed by affluent diners and tourists. There was active civic debate about whether the site should even be preserved. I found a gated entrance opening to a dark staircase. At its end were tunnels into the original bomb shelter. There one could hear the tape in the dimly lit shelter where many peace activists once huddled. A vinyl record copy sits in its jacket unnoticed in the hotel's lobby amid throngs of wandering tourists and children.

Nixon never ended his quest for a victory protecting U.S. interests, including a face-saving Korea-like partition of Vietnam in which American flags would fly over the propped-up remains of the Saigon regime. On April 6, 1975, the hawkish Democratic senator Henry M. "Scoop" Jackson from Washington State revealed that Nixon had worked out "secret agreements" to supply Saigon with unspecified military assistance in the future. The White House denied Jackson's charges but admitted that Nixon had written privately to General Thieu affirming that he would "react vigorously to major violations" of the Paris Peace Accords.

Many of us who had worked so hard to end the war wondered whether the fall of Indochina before the 1976 election of Jimmy Carter would lead to real change, a serious reordering of national priorities, or would his election see the resurgence of the serpent in the garden?

The political effect of the Watergate hearings finally led Nixon to board his helicopter and fly away on August 9, 1974, turning over the presidency to Vice President Gerald Ford. In February 1975, the hard-line secretary of state Henry Kissinger urged Ford to resume the bombing in the face of the Vietnamese offensive in Phuoc Long Province near Cambodia from mid-December through early January. Ford declined to launch a counteroffensive, both because he had never agreed to approve such a step and because of overwhelming opposition from the Congress and public opinion. The new president, a former congressman himself, knew he lacked the votes and rightly feared that a unilateral resumption of the bombing would ignite a public furor at home, with national elections just a year away.

Did the Vietnam War end because America lost its fighting spirit and succumbed to liberal media and Democratic politicians, as most neoconservatives and their military allies still insist today? Or was it lost because of the superior military firepower of the North Vietnamese and their National Liberation Front comrades in the South, as some on the left insist? What role did the peace movement play in ending the war? Were the thousands of protests only a sideshow in a larger power struggle, a noise signifying nothing in the final outcome? Worse, as nearly all Republicans and even some Democrats charge, did the peace movement actually delay peace by not supporting Hubert Humphrey and thus caus-

ing him to lose by less than 1 percent in the 1968 presidential
election?

Measuring outcomes is far from simple. In Humphrey's
case, many—including myself—argue that if the vice president had broken with Johnson and declared his preference for
a Johnson-backed bombing halt and a negotiated settlement a
few weeks earlier, he would have reversed the gap from trail-
ing by double digits to take the lead at the end. The evidence
of Nixon's conspiring with Saigon to scuttle the talks, delay-
ing a late-hour diplomatic agreement, is persuasive. On the
other hand, George Wallace won 13 percent of the national
vote, leaving the doves well behind the hawks in the polling.

The charge that the liberal Left elected Nixon by defect-
ing from Humphrey is harder to refute. The closing of the gap
toward the end suggests that huge numbers of voters were
switching to Humphrey in October, refuting the suspicion of
mass defections. But it is true that many on the left refused
to vote for Humphrey out of our own nihilism and despair.
The claim by some that there was no real difference between
Nixon and Humphrey is without foundation, just like Ralph
Nader's 2000 denial of any difference between Al Gore and
George W. Bush. Dogmatic fealty to principles over pragma-
tism, or emotions over a calculated strategy, resulted in conservative, militaristic outcomes in both elections. The peace
movement was short on political experience as well as wisdom.

The insistence by some that the war was won by the Vietnamese armed struggle alone is oversimplified. Obviously the
Vietnamese resistance, from Dien Bien Phu in 1954 to the fall
of Saigon in 1975, was a continuous battle in arms. But the

evidence shows the Vietnamese employed a deliberately co-ordinated and brilliantly executed strategy of simultaneously waging political, diplomatic, and armed struggle.

There is no doubt the peace movement was crucial to the political battlegrounds. Those Americans who waved National Liberation Front flags were if anything counterproductive in their messaging, but they never accounted for more than a tiny fraction of the demonstrators opposed to the war. Our accomplishments were real by any measure: we organized and legitimized public protest for the first time since the suffocations of McCarthyism, our numbers growing into the millions. The GI movement had a deterrent effect on U.S. military escalation, despite Nixon's efforts to fabricate and fund Republican veterans' groups. We were the main factor in ending the military draft and legislating the eighteen-year-old vote for the first time since 1945. We triggered the so-called credibility gap by relentless exposure of military secrets from My Lai to the Cambodian "incursion" to secret saturation bombings and torture of Vietnamese prisoners. While our movement in legend and memory is sometimes limited to sound and fury, our political effect should be remembered for the true importance it had. The peace movement was the core opposition force as the number of Americans who called Vietnam a "mistake" rose to majority proportions. Peace activists were the front-line ground troops in the McCarthy, Kennedy, and McGovern campaigns, realigning American politics to include a mass-based bloc of peace voters that could not be ignored. Claims that we "aided the enemy" are based on the false notion that the American public would have supported any means whatsoever, any cost in blood or taxes, to achieve the impossible goal of making Hanoi surrender. Never before in American history had a peace movement had such an impact. Failure to recognize the historic role of the Vietnam peace movement is a dangerous denial bordering on delusion. It also is a wholly unnecessary self-inflicted wound, a wound that without reconciliation and a rigorous and honest accounting will refuse to heal.

After the 1975 fall of Saigon came a long-awaited Liberal Moment. Jimmy Carter was elected president to succeed Gerald Ford, elevate the civil rights movement, clear the fetid air of the poisonous Nixon crimes, and pardon America's thousands of draft resisters. Carter and Zbigniew Brzezinski, his national security advisor, also sought to restore America's prestige in the world, badly tarnished by its Vietnam misadventure. The old demon of Communism could no longer be used as the glue that held together the bipartisan Cold War consensus. Nixon had smashed it by recognizing Mao's China and by encouraging détente with Leonid Brezhnev's Soviet Union. Something new was needed. Carter and Brzezinski raised the banner of human rights, and it would be beneath this sign that a new rationale would be presented to the American people for renewed U.S. meddling in other countries' affairs. The conceit of safeguarding human rights while spreading democracy would be the unacknowledged gift bequeathed to President Reagan and his hard-line neocons. They would use it as a fig leaf rationale to justify the American imperium. It would be the stake that would be driven through the heart of a new condition called the Vietnam Syndrome. Both neoliberals and neoconservatives correctly feared that the vast majority of the nation's citizens had developed a profound aversion to the use of American troops abroad. They were right: the trauma of the Vietnam War and the peace movement had inoculated many Americans against the notion that we ought to be the constable policing the world.

The 1979 kidnapping of American diplomats in Iran by followers of Ayatollah Ruhollah Khomeini, who had overthrown the shah, caused a backlash among many Americans against Carter, however, and propelled former California governor Ronald Reagan into the White House. Cold War winds began to blow against alleged Communist conspiracies in Central America. Seventy thousand would die in the American-fostered conflict in El Salvador, along with thirty thousand in the Contra war to overthrow the Sandinistas in Nicaragua. Reagan himself came close to impeachment proceedings over charges of secretly and illegally authorizing the buying of weapons for the Contra terrorists with drug money from the ghettos of Los Angeles. Elliott Abrams, his assistant secretary of state for inter-American affairs, pled guilty to two misdemeanors for withholding information from Congress but was pardoned by Reagan's successor, George H. W. Bush. The Liberal Moment soon faded away. The tom-toms of the reactionary surge were beating ever more loudly. Right-wing diehards would use the victorious peace movement and its veterans as a scapegoat for the manifest failures of American adventurism. Repeated attempts to brand us as traitors and unpatriotic would persist, and efforts would be mounted to write us out of the official history—history we had helped make, at much cost and sacrifice.

4

TEN YEARS AGO, during Christmas 2007, I traveled with my wife, Barbara Williams, and our seven-year-old son, Liam, to Vietnam, for the first time in thirty-two years. I was feeling a deep need to see the place once more, regretting having withdrawn from a country I had visited four times during the height of the war. I wanted to understand the long-term lessons and, on a personal basis, track down the Vietnamese guides and translators, men and women, who assumed an ideological faith in the American "people" they escorted through ruins inflicted by the American "enemy." After the war, they would become important bridges, involved in the U.S.-Vietnam diplomatic recognition and efforts at reconciliation. How had their world changed? How much had they unified with those who fought, lost, and suffered on the American side? Most of them were survivors of the French and American wars and would be in their eighties by now. Were many still alive? How had they suffered? After the exuberance at their military victory and sudden reunification after 1975, how had they adjusted to a Vietnam without war? Or had nothing changed due to the two subsequent wars with China?

Vietnam's consul in San Francisco, Chau Do, told me that

many of these old revolutionaries were alive, excited by my imminent return and inquiring whom I wanted to see. I told him that my closest and oldest Vietnamese friend was a poet, musician, and translator, Do Xuan Oanh, who was perhaps forty in those days. "I can help you find him," Chau replied with a smile. "He's my dad."

Before I would reunite with these old friends and contacts, however, I plunged into the shocking contrasts between past and present in Hanoi. Between the period during which I made four unauthorized visits to Hanoi—from Christmas 1965 to November 1972—and the present day. The wartime city in those early days was unlit and ghostly. Most people had been evacuated to the countryside. Air-raid sirens and public-safety broadcasts were the only urban sounds. There was no economic development beyond the construction of pontoon bridges to replace bridges bombed by the Americans. The only motorized vehicles were military ones. Most residents rode bicycles or carried their meager wares on bamboo poles across their shoulders. Water buffalo pulled the heavier loads. To outward appearances, General Curtis LeMay's plan to bomb Vietnam back to the Stone Age was on track.

Now, suddenly, it seemed to me, it was Christmas 2007 and Vietnam was ablaze with festive holiday lights, from Hanoi to Ho Chi Minh City. Though billboards of Ho Chi Minh were pervasive, the most ubiquitous bearded one this Christmas season was Santa Claus, beckoning shoppers from department store doorways, seen incongruously riding motorbikes, waving to little children. Spectacular strings of red and green lights festooned the streets and stores, blinking at thousands of Vietnamese who rolled along on bicycles and motorbikes and parted smoothly like schools of fish around pedestrians crossing the street. Restaurant-goers applauded Christmas carols sung by young Vietnamese women strapped in Heineken girls sashes. None of this was about Jesus—Christmas was not a native tradition in this Buddhist and secular Marxist country—it was all about corporate branding. The fancy Diamond department store next to Independence Palace was filled with shoppers, gawkers, and Santas wandering the aisles of Lego, Calvin Klein, Victoria's Secret, Nike, Converse, Estée Lauder, Ferragamo, and Bally. The nearby Saigon Centre bore a billboard proclaiming, "More Shops, More Life."

Far be it from me to question the desire of the Vietnamese to share our globalized consumer culture like everyone else, or to reject their aspiration to be the next Asian Tiger, or freeze them in memory as icons of selfless revolutionaries. Gentrification and consumerism, after all, have destroyed the character of my favorite American haunts, too, like North Beach, Berkeley, Venice, and Aspen. It seems to be the way of the world.

As I walked through the busy Christmas streets, however, I was gripped by the question of why the Vietnam War was necessary in the first place. Why kill, maim, and uproot millions of Vietnamese if the outcome was a consumer wonderland approved by the country's still-undefeated Communist Party? The whole wretched American rationale for the war, that Vietnam was a dangerous domino, a pawn in the Cold War, seemed so painfully wrong. Was there any connection between destroying so much life and causing the Vietnamese to go Christmas shopping? Would the same outcome—a one-party socialist government leading a market economy—have occurred in any event, without the destruction? Now that U.S. naval ships were paying peaceful visits to Da Nang, this question nagged at me: was it possible that Marxism and nationalism had won the war but that capitalism and nationalism won the peace?

Those who still believe Vietnam was a "necessary" war must take pleasure at seeing that country in the camp of corporate neoliberalism. A proud new member of the World Trade Organization (WTO), Vietnam in 2007 welcomed a $1 billion Intel project to Ho Chi Minh City, and accepted the wholesale privatization of telecommunications and other industries.

Some in Hanoi were dismayed by all of this. An American expatriate, Gerry Herman, a former antiwar activist turned businessman and film distributor who has lived in Vietnam for fifteen years, told me that the Vietnamese were so desperately eager to normalize relations with the United States that they accepted the most liberal market reforms of any developing country. Having some internal knowledge of the trade negotiations, he told me bitterly that Vietnam was "blackmailed" by the U.S. negotiators. To gain export markets for their textiles, shoes, and seafood, the Vietnamese had slashed subsidies and opened markets in banking, insurance, services, and advertising to private corporations. For Herman, the distressing prospect was that Vietnam would follow the failed model of the Philippines, not the more successful Asian Tigers whose development benefited from government subsidies.

China, Herman said, got a better deal than Vietnam, winning twenty years of protection for its telecommunications industry. "The American negotiators said to Vietnam that they were beaten by the Chinese on certain issues and would never do it again, and Vietnam could take the deal or leave it." (The problem continues today with the Trans-Pacific Partnership Agreement [TPP], pending congressional approval as of this writing. Two American expatriates living in Vietnam told me, "If Vietnam ratifies the TPP, it will begin to lose elements of its national sovereignty in five years. Laws and regulations enacted by the government of Vietnam may be overpowered, overridden, and replaced by provisions of the TPP.") The Americans, in deference to domestic political pressure, even demanded market access for Harley-Davidson, against the Vietnamese complaint that Harleys, larger and faster than other brands, would worsen the high accident rates on their narrow, congested roads. "The Vietnamese negotiator broke down in tears" over the Harley concession, Herman said. I suddenly remembered the cynical 1960s strategy of Harvard's Samuel Huntington, who approvingly predicted that forced urbanization would transform the Vietnamese into a "Honda culture." It was coming true before my eyes, with the Honda Dream motorcycle and, sooner or later, the Harley. As a Vietnamese named Pham Thong Long blogged, "I have only one dream is buy one of brand new Harley-Davidson, now I waiting for Harley-Davidson dealer to open in Saigon. I need a Fatboy."

It is difficult to discern the truth across these cultural divides. Leftist scholars like the late Gabriel Kolko had predicted the disintegration of the Vietnamese Communist Party for decades, but the political situation in the country is by most accounts stable, even improved.

Thao Griffiths, a thirty-year-old who directed the Hanoi office of Vietnam Veterans of America, reminded me of certain fundamentals on my first day adjusting to the new Hanoi. "Since thirty years ago when you were first here, we have motorbikes in addition to bicycles, cell phones more than land lines, an Internet, and most of our population, like myself, were born after the wars. This has been a time to catch up in peace." As for Hanoi's accepting the WTO, Thao said, "We knew the mechanism was not fair, but the strategic reason is we had to get accepted inside. We didn't really have 'normal' economic relations with the United States until 2006, for four decades. Even last year, Bush was saying America should have stayed the course in Vietnam."

Thao herself reflected postwar Vietnam: fluent in English and a former Fulbright scholar, she spent two years at the Vietnam Veterans' office in Washington, DC, deeply involved in the normalization process. She has translated for Hillary Clinton, arranged tours for multiple American visitors, negotiated with Boeing, and helped to oversee a range of social service and educational projects, including programs to respect and protect Agent Orange victims, both Vietnamese and American. She has two children with her Australian husband, Patrick, a researcher for the United Nations. Her little boy, Liem, immediately befriended our seven-year-old Liam on walks, shopping trips, sleepovers, and trips to fabled Ha Long Bay.

Vietnam's annual economic growth of 7 to 8 percent in recent years has been significant, though it has come at the price of rising inequalities, a pattern in many other countries under neoliberalism. Per capita GDP rose from $200 in 1993 to $835 at the time of my 2007 visit. That was still less than $2 a day for most Vietnamese, but it came close to removing Vietnam from the World Bank's category of the poorest nations. The Vietnamese government estimated foreign direct investment at $13 billion in 2007, its highest investors being South Korea, the British Virgin Islands, a conduit for offshore Hong Kong money, and Singapore. Poverty fell from 58 percent to 20 percent, though the majority of ethnic minorities and rural Vietnamese still lived in poverty, and growth had created catastrophic problems of infrastructure, traffic congestion, and pollution.

The Laodong Party introduced its drastic *doi moi* market policies in 1986, a "renovation" plan that opened doors to private foreign investment and a Gorbachev-style internal perestroika. An exhaustive European study concluded in 2006 that a remarkable result of the doi moi reforms had been "the absence of organized social opposition among workers, peasants and youth. They are generally content with their growing economic opportunities."

Of course, Vietnam was a one-party state that closely monitored the Internet and pockets of dissent among religious and ethnic groups. But the institutional controls had been steadily relaxed since the 1970s, with none of the uprisings that accompanied the fall of Soviet or Eastern European Communism. Nor had there been a Tiananmen Square revolt in Hanoi. "Democratic debate within the party and within the National Assembly, as well as personal freedoms, have made much progress since the war," observed John McAuliff, a reconstruction specialist who has made fifty trips to the country. "It's true that it wouldn't be wise to stand up on a soapbox and advocate the overthrow of the government," said Lady Borton, a longtime American expatriate and translator in Hanoi. "But there is widespread criticism of the party leaders on all levels in private and in the press." She called such leaders "bulldogs." In an observation I shared, Borton described Vietnam as "a place of constant talk, all the time, and they talk freely."

Kent Wong, the director of UCLA's labor studies center, discerned a positive spirit among Vietnam's working class based on taking several union delegations to Vietnam during the last five years. "I've seen poverty in many developing countries, and Vietnam is different. There are no shantytowns," Wong said. Vietnamese unions, Wong acknowledged, are not constituted as adversarial bargaining units, but the many members he has interviewed have high morale. "Four years ago when I was there, they had a plan to organize 1 million more workers in the public sector, and they actually met the goal," he said. Wide income disparities prevailed in the private sector, but inequalities in the public sector were less pronounced. Wong, who wanted to turn the AFL-CIO away from its lingering Cold War and CIA-financed heritage of anti-Communism toward Vietnam and China, was working to build direct worker-to-worker relationships to foster labor solidarity strategies in the age of globalization.

To make sense of the contradictions between Vietnam's

grinding poverty and rising affluence, between defeating Americans in war but joining the WTO in peace, one must consider Vietnam's history. Perhaps no country in the modern world has suffered the sorrows of war more heavily and for a longer consecutive period than Vietnam. Leaving out the century of French colonialism, the Vietnamese survived, even prevailed, during the Japanese occupation in World War II, the nine-year war against French reconquest (365,000 battle deaths), the fifteen-year war with the Americans (2.1 million battle deaths), and the ten-year war with Pol Pot's Cambodia and China in the 1980s. Millions of Vietnamese died of famine or lived with hunger and deprivation as everyday experiences. After the American war, unexploded bombs and landmines killed at least 38,000 more Vietnamese, and countless numbers continue to live with the deformities resulting from 20 million gallons of dioxin-laced Agent Orange and other defoliants. Their sufferings are beyond imagination.

All this sacrifice was accepted as either a duty in the war for independence or a reality to be accepted and survived. The deep personalized pain of Vietnamese killing one another, not simply the foreign invaders, accompanied it. At least 185,000 Saigon soldiers died, for example, dishonored as having cast their lot with the losing side.

Here, perhaps, is the explanation for Vietnam's intense two-decade quest to achieve something resembling a normal life, to avoid exclusion from the world community. This memory of trauma is why they believe normalization with the United States, accession to the WTO, and a nonpermanent seat on the UN Security Council are strategic "victories" on a long road to recovery. It is a matter of great pride that a Vietnamese Bronze Age drum is placed at the entrance to the UN Security Council today.

"'No More War' was the lesson after Vietnam for our people," said Bao Ninh, author of *The Sorrow of War*, a 1993 antiwar novel ranking in my mind with the classics of Erich Maria Remarque, Joseph Heller, Kurt Vonnegut, Norman Mailer, and, among Vietnam War veterans, Tim O'Brien and Philip Caputo, to name only two of the most well known. We visited Ninh one evening at his Hanoi residence, where he and his wife received us with tea, fruit, and cake. His first floor was a bright reception room with a couch, chairs and, in one corner, a motorbike. Ninh's novel was initially banned by state censors for allegedly undermining the national consensus that the war had been patriotic, victorious, and glorious. But under doi moi the book gained a huge audience in Vietnamese and other languages, and was in development to be produced as a film.

When he was fifteen, Ninh saw his first American. It was John McCain, parachuting from his burning fighter-bomber into Truc Bach Lake in Hanoi after destroying a power plant. Ninh watched as McCain, drowning with two broken arms, was pulled from the lake by a local fisherman at a spot marked by a small monument today. Ninh later joined the army to fight in South Vietnam, was among the soldiers who liberated Saigon in 1975, and was assigned to search for the decomposing bodies of dead soldiers after the war. His book is more about man's inhumanity to man than a tale of triumphant revolution. I was stunned by the jacket's description of Ninh as one of only ten survivors of a youth brigade of five hundred. With a laugh, he surprised me by saying the numbers were made up by his American publisher, Pantheon. "Not only governments but soldiers themselves make up war stories, too," he laughed again, reminding me of sardonic American Vietnam veterans. "I like writing. I write about what I know. I wanted to tell a soldier's story, not a political or ideological one."

Ninh visited the United States in 1998 with other Vietnamese writers, gaining a vivid impression of U.S. diversity, including surprise at how many Americans were "quite fat." That aside, even in conservative towns like Missoula, Montana, he found Vietnam memorials and town officials who were veterans like himself. Ninh came away impressed that so many Americans still "remembered, discussed, and agonized over Vietnam," and formed the opinion that this memory of Vietnam could be "a tower of strength from the past" on which to build better relations in the future. Beneath his friendly bearing, Ninh carried the scars and guilt only some war veterans are capable of expressing. The most painful, perhaps, was his "sorrow at having survived," the belief that the very best of his generation had died for Vietnam's present peace. "Look carefully now at the peace we have, painful, bitter, and sad. And look who won the war. To win, martyrs had sacrificed their lives in order that others might survive. Not a new phenomenon, true. But those still living to know that the kindest, most worthy people have all fallen away, or even been tortured, humiliated before being killed, or buried and wiped away by the machinery of war, then this beautiful landscape of calm and peace is an appalling paradox."

Ninh was repelled by Vietnam's Marxist postwar policies. "In the war, I had lived like an animal. Now I couldn't
stand this [the peace]. Some Americans may sympathize with
Communism but I lived under it and couldn't stand it. Every-
body was fed up with the hardship. That's what led to the
doi moi in the eighties." One of Bao Ninh's sons was now
making millions in the global high-tech industry and traveled
frequently to the United States. It's not the future he fought
for at the same age, he said, but he was proud and happy for
his son. "We Vietnamese are not like North Korea or China.
If Communism doesn't work, we move on. But North Korea,
for example, has a very tough time because they keep going
on with Communism."

Not many Vietnamese today reflect on the war with America with Bao Ninh's profound cynicism, because that would
mean questioning much of their country's very identity,
somewhat like an American questioning the Indian wars or
the Revolution. Rather, the American war is perceived as a
necessity forced on Vietnam by invading powers, as had happened for more than a thousand years, beginning with the
Chinese. Vietnamese take pride in having defeated so many
great powers and feel deeply about their losses. There is a
suppressed anger at their being willing to join the search for
American MIAs while the U.S. government and Monsanto
refuse to take significant responsibility for Agent Orange.

The question is whether the future, aside from the obvi-
ous advantages of peace, will be worth the sacrifices of the
past. Is the period of anticolonial revolution—which Vietnam
symbolized and which so dominated our thinking in the six-

ties and beyond—becoming an obsolete memory in the era of globalization? Has the promise of those inspiring revolutions faded with the decline of naked colonialism and the emergence of so many corrupt authoritarianisms in the Third World? Or are the supposedly scientific models of history long embraced by the Left being replaced with a kind of chaos theory of unpredictability? Is this all that was ever possible?

Perhaps this was why I stayed away so long but had to return after so many decades. Much as I still opposed war and imperialism, from Vietnam to Iraq, I no longer expected joyous endings. I wanted to see my oldest acquaintances in Vietnam for personal reasons but also as guides in sorting out these troubling questions. I call these people, now in their eighties, Vietnam's old revolutionary generation. Their roots went back nearly a century, to young Ho Chi Minh's odyssey to the West—in particular, France and America—to study the spirit of republican revolutions for lessons he might bring home.

Ho, then known as Nguyen Ai Quoc, presented a petition to the 1919 Versailles conference asking for Vietnam's inclusion in the call for self-determination. There he learned that Woodrow Wilson's Fourteen Points did not apply to the colonies. In the period of the Russian Revolution, Ho was waiting tables in Harlem and making diary notes on the lynchings of African Americans. He embraced Marxism-Leninism because of Lenin's opposition to colonialism. Twenty-five years later, Ho collaborated with American intelligence agents in resisting the Japanese occupation. Then he cited the American Declaration of Independence in declaring Vietnam's freedom in 1945. From long tradition grew the practical and even sentimental belief that the "American people," in Walt Whitman's mythic invocation, could be appealed to against American imperialism.

Thus arose Viet-My (Vietnamese-American) solidarity committees and cultural exchanges from the very beginnings of the war with the United States, staffed by bright young Vietnamese who were asked to host American wartime visitors and in the process learned more about American culture and politics. Now long retired, many of these old revolutionaries went on after the war to become diplomats and ambassadors to European countries. In 2007, many in Hanoi still arose at 5:30 for morning exercises at the Flying Dragon Club, an old building with a curved roof, then, with bodies limber and spirits balanced, went out for tea and conversation. In general, the old revolutionaries were busy, active in community affairs, proud and nationalistic, and shared with me their unanimous sense that Vietnam had become too materialistic and acquisitive. "The new generation lacks a balanced approach," said eighty-one-year-old Nguyen Ngoc Dung, who ran shelters for street children in Ho Chi Minh City. "The situation is out of balance," said another. "They are not looking—how do you say?—at the other side of the coin."

Dung was a former deputy to the most well known of the old revolutionaries, eighty-one-year-old Nguyen Thi Binh, who presided over the Peace and Development Foundation in Hanoi. During the war, "Madame Binh," as she was known, was a striking global icon and nemesis denounced by Henry Kissinger in the Paris peace negotiations. When she welcomed me for tea, she seemed smaller than the woman I remembered, but her energy remained vibrant. The formality of the reunion was derailed by the arrival of the "two Liams," arm in arm. They sat on Binh's grandmotherly lap while she held forth on the challenges of healing the damage of Agent Orange and developing Vietnam past the status of other poor countries. She showed a keen interest in sponsoring workshops with critics of globalization. Meanwhile, the two little Liams lobbied to be taken to the local Lego franchise.

On another morning, the sudden arrival of an older man in a blue windbreaker surprised me. He walked toward me, peering carefully through wide spectacles. "Do you remember who I am?" he asked with an expectant look. Then he held before me a black-and-white photo of myself, ten pounds lighter and thirty-five years younger, staring at Vietnamese graves, notebook in hand. The man with glasses was Pham Khac Lam, an interpreter and photographer whom I last saw in 1972 deep within a cave in rural North Vietnam. Lam, now seventy-seven, was the top assistant to General Vo Nguyen Giap in preparing the battle plan for Dien Bien Phu in 1954. His father was a mandarin advisor to Emperor Bao Dai, the last Vietnamese monarch. Lam's father is said to have written Bao Dai's abdication speech in 1945. Lam, in other words, grew up in the absolute center of Vietnamese anticolonialism, joined the solidarity committees during the American war, and participated in the postwar process as director of the country's first television network. He was part of the 2005 Rose Garden ceremonies when Vietnam's Prime Minister Pham Van Khai met President George W. Bush. He takes modest credit for the idea of flying both the Vietnamese and U.S. flags on the stretch limousine carrying Hanoi officials to the White House door. And he once told Civil War buff Ted Turner, who opened media relations between CNN and Hanoi, that "it was important to let the past be 'gone with the wind.'" Turner generously sold Lam the rights to broadcast CNN for a nickel.

Lam edited *Viet-My*, a glossy magazine devoted to promotional reports on commercial and diplomatic ties with the United States, including critical commentary on issues like Agent Orange. Occasionally Lam inserted a strategic analysis of the U.S. quandary in Iraq, buried amid advertisements beckoning tourists to such attractions as health clubs at the beach. How did he really feel, I wondered, about the world he had done so much to shape? Lam seemed relaxed and diplomatic. His duties have included welcoming former Saigon dictator Nguyen Cao Ky, who had visited Hanoi frequently in recent years, against vociferous complaints from Vietnamese exiles in America. "Ky said he always wanted to unify Vietnam, so I have to salute him," Lam said wryly. On the question of his country's deepening inequalities, however, Lam parted from the optimistic party line. "The government is trying to reduce poverty, but it's already a reality. The rich are getting richer because they have the means. And the poor don't. We are better off materially, but not mentally, ethically," he said, brushing his forehead.

The world had changed all around him, from the caves of resistance to welcomes in the Rose Garden, from Dien Bien Phu to the global media stage. The geopolitical balance was altered forever with no more Soviet Union or "socialist camp" and tensions simmering beneath the "fraternal relations" with China. "We and the Chinese used to call each other comrade; now it's mister," he reflected.

The most ironic piece of the puzzle before me was falling into place. While it could not be said explicitly—and while Vietnam inevitably would strive to maintain close and correct relations with China, its giant northern neighbor—the United States could serve as a strategic balance in Asia for Hanoi, while Vietnam served as a check on the expanding Chinese power Washington fears most. Ironically, it's becoming the domino theory in reverse.

Finally, I visited my oldest friend, Do Xuan Oanh, who had first greeted me at Hanoi's airport on a December day forty-two years before. I had been told that he went through a "bitter period" after postwar retirement but was now feeling better, having recently translated into English an edition of Vietnamese women's poetry. Oanh lived alone, his wife having died after many years of illness and his three sons all abroad. My memory of Oanh was that he had loved America in his particular way. For example, after learning English from the BBC, he translated Mark Twain's *Huckleberry Finn* into Vietnamese, a massive challenge. A musician, he could sing many American protest songs. A romantic, he wept easily and became close to many Americans.

Now, in a carload of old revolutionaries, I traveled along a narrow cement path past a few stone houses until we came to the gate of Oanh's home of fifty years. He was standing waiting in the doorway, a thin shadow of the man I remembered.

Taking my hand, he led me into a windowless room where a couch and piano were the most prominent fixtures. There were alcoves for painting and a kitchen. We sat and looked at each other. He held my hand on his knee, while the others sat in a quiet circle. It was more a final visit, a good-bye, than a time to renew old conversations.

"Do you want some booze?" Oanh asked with a low chuckle, pointing to a half bottle of Jim Beam. I demurred. Oanh seemed fit and energetic for an eighty-five-year-old. My wife, Barbara, asked if he would play the piano, and he performed an original piece in a classic European style. He gave me a copy of the song, signed to his "precious friend," and a small carving of a beautiful Vietnamese woman carrying a student briefcase, which he said reminded him of his wife "before the revolution." He repeated the phrase and then relaxed. Gradually, the others began to reminisce about the old days. I wondered if we would ever meet again. I remembered an e-mail I'd received from Oanh's son in San Francisco: "I believe God assigned my father and myself to serve the American people." His son would come for a visit in the summer, Oanh said.

We walked back along the dark path to the street filled with motorbikes and strolling couples out for coffee. Oanh looked at me intently, pointing a finger for emphasis. "Nothing can be predicted," he said as we parted. That seemed true of my life experience.

The very nature of the world, and the world of revolutions, had changed unimaginably since 1965, when I first joined the antiwar movement. The most unnerving, and rarely discussed, changes took place within the China-Vietnam-

American triangle of history. During the fifties, U.S. politics were dominated by McCarthyism and the charged question "Who lost China?" Liberals were discredited, diplomatic careers derailed, and public hysteria over "yellow hordes" inflated. Vietnam was defined as a vanguard of the Yellow Peril crossing the Pacific, despite the awkward fact that China and Vietnam were historic enemies and that Vietnam enjoyed close ties with the Soviet Union, China's rival in Cold War power politics.

The Chinese Cultural Revolution, launched in 1966, upended these relationships overnight. Mao Zedong called on the Chinese younger generation to rise up against the alleged corruption and opportunism of the party members among their own parents. The feverish Red Guards were unleashed as shock troops everywhere, exhorted by Mao "to bombard the headquarters" of status quo institutions. One thousand eight hundred people were killed in Beijing alone from August to September 1966, according to a later party analysis. From the new "revolutionary" perspective, even Vietnam itself was suspected of harboring "revisionism" because of its dependence on Soviet weapons, advisors, foreign aid, and diplomats. To the Chinese, the "main enemy" in the world was the same Soviet revisionism which, among other tainted policies, favored a negotiated settlement of the Vietnam War through an unspecified détente between Washington and Moscow. Indeed, there were plenty of machinations attempted by the Nixon administration to divide and conquer the "socialist camp," but that camp was already strained to the maximum by the differences between Beijing and Moscow.

In the United States and Europe, left-wing intellectuals

became Maoists taking the side of the Cultural Revolution and adopting the most extreme and divisive positions on the left. Towering Paris luminaries like Michel Foucault, Jean-Paul Sartre, and Jean-Luc Godard waved the banner and the *Little Red Book* of Mao. The Chairman's phrase "Revolution is not a dinner party" was understood as a defense of going to any extremes in service to the goal of a purified revolution and state. Intellectuals like Alan Badieu celebrated violent tactics like combative "terroristic nihilism." The Left across the world was riven by sectarian strife. The peace movement and American progressives were caught in the crossfire. How this antagonism could possibly help end the war in Vietnam was the subject of deep puzzlement and paralysis.

What finally occurred was the devolution of Cambodia's Khmer Rouge, whose own leaders were trained by Maoist intellectuals in French academies before they morphed into the sectarian madness of the notorious killing fields, in which more than 1 million people were executed or forced to abandon their "bourgeois privileges" by marching into the countryside far from their families.

One of the first victims of the Red Guard purges was Xi Jinping, the current president of China, whose father was tossed out as an "enemy of the revolution" when Xi was thirteen years old. The young Xi spent seven years assigned to a rural village where he sometimes was forced to clean latrines and wear a cone-shaped hat. One of his sisters died in the upheaval. Xi's father, who was a vice premier, was dispatched to factory labor. Xi ultimately was permitted to see his father in 1952, when the Chinese government arranged a reunion.

"The father, battered and disoriented after years of isolation and interrogation," could not even recognize Xi or his brother, according to reporters Chris Buckley and Didi Kirsten Tatlow's account in the *New York Times*.

If the Chinese Cultural Revolution was "unpredictable," to cite my Vietnamese friend Oanh's admonition, the politics of the Khmer Rouge conformed to the worst stereotypes of Communism to be found in George Orwell or Arthur Koestler. After Kissinger and Nixon's brutalist policies had shattered the Cambodian state, the Khmer Rouge seized power in place of the neutralist King Norodom Sihanouk and commenced the destruction of Cambodia in April 1970. Then, in another unpredictable twist, three years after the end of the Vietnam War, the Vietnamese armed forces invaded and occupied Cambodia in December 1978 to destroy the Khmer Rouge. Then there came a bloody border war in 1979 between China and Vietnam before China decided to pull its troops back.

Nothing was predictable. As noted, the United States and Vietnam fully normalized their relations on July 11, 1995, with Thao Griffiths translating and Mr. Lam in charge of the media. A decade later, a Pew poll showed 78 percent of the Vietnamese people held a favorable view of the United States. Today, with the Chinese and Vietnamese fleets contesting each other in the South China Sea, with several militaries on standby, with Washington a de facto ally of Vietnam as a new Cold War with China unfolds, who can possibly predict the next phase of our country's tortured history with Vietnam? And how can the historical memory of the antiwar movement of 1965–75 avoid greater distortion?

What is clear is that America has a haunted memory of those years expressed as a desire for "No More Vietnams" and a rejection of any notion of being the world's policeman. Most Americans favor negotiated political solutions over Vietnam-style intervention by force. It's reassuring that most Americans also favor reconciliation with Vietnam, including joint programs to remove unexploded bombs and mitigate the long-range health impacts of Agent Orange in that country's soil and waterways. A surprising level of goodwill continues to sustain the bilateral relationship. And this atmosphere is due in no small part to the long-standing policy of the Vietnamese to distinguish between what they long have called the "American government policy" and "the American people."

The phrasing sounds like a cliché, or outright propaganda. The implied faith in "the American people" is beyond comprehension to any serious skeptic or student of how U.S. history is drenched in racism and nineteenth-century colonialism. "The American people" are stained with guilt, many critics might justifiably say. As a practical matter, how could any of the Vietnamese victims, we might ask, forgive the American aggressors and thank us for our "democratic traditions"? But the same question could be asked about any of the American victims of Vietnamese violence, including Senator McCain, whose cooperation with his former captors has been essential to postwar reconciliation. The mutuality of healing is a process many have chosen on both sides.

The distinction between the American government and America's people is more than a party line. It is evident on a human and verifiable level today among the thousands of participants in cultural exchanges and tourist travel between America and Vietnam. Vietnam veterans are drawn with their families back to old battlefields where they find themselves bonding with their former enemies, drinking tea and story-telling, surprised at how welcoming and hospitable the Viet-namese seem to be. Why this is so is an enduring mystery.

One clue comes from the experience of the early antiwar movement. "The Vietnamese taught us to reach out to every-one," recalled Vivian Rothstein, a longtime union organizer in Los Angeles who traveled to Hanoi in 1967 and met the Vietnamese again many years later at an international con-ference in Canada. "Obviously, it made no sense to antago-nize us or guilt-trip us in meetings intended to reach a greater understanding," Rothstein said. By comparison, she will never forget the petty rivalries, fighting among factions, and self-hatred that so often consumed the antiwar movement itself. The Vietnamese "imparted to us a democratic idea, the idea of trying to connect with every single person of whatever background in order for them to build stronger support for ending the war. I do think it affected our thinking about our-selves and our movement, too." She compared that approach with the alienated styles of so many late-sixties radicals mari-nated in bitterness, self-hate, isolation, and shame over white-skin privilege. "What kind of organizing approach is that?"

To look at a current example, there is a vast distance be-tween the Vietnamese distinction between "government" and "people" and the opposite approach of ISIS, which con-demns wholesale the "infidel" populations of the non-Muslim world. It is impossible to imagine the Vietnamese shooting up and suicide-bombing scores of French twenty-somethings as a matter of military and political strategy. Both the present generation of North African jihadists and the Vietnamese share a past legacy of oppression and suffering imposed on them by the French. Yet their responses, and even their world-views, could not be more different. The Vietnamese never relied upon the American peace movement to deliver a victory for them, as long insisted by American neoconservatives. But they did appeal to America's democratic heritage, culture, and mechanisms, however paltry, of redress. The war revealed that the ultimate question was between empire and democracy. The peace movement learned to make the right choice.

The Vietnamese in those days already knew plenty about the American soldiers on their bases, in the markets, bars, and brothels on the streets of Saigon, or on the other side of barbed concertina wire. But now we were a new variety of innocent Americans they tried to understand. Of course the Vietnamese could be ruthless in war, stereotyped as a fanatical Yellow Peril. Of course they were engaged in an information war and guerrilla war, not in building friendship circles, so, yes, they planted poisoned traps in the jungle and carried out many tactics that were intrinsically cruel, and often effective.

Yet among about two hundred American peace activists who visited Hanoi in the years 1965 through 1975, there was a common sense that the Vietnamese had genuinely warm feelings toward "the American people" as opposed to the American government. This sentiment was completely unlike that of the more chauvinist Chinese and Koreans who invaded the Korean peninsula, or that of Al Qaeda or ISIS today. Centuries of oppression hardens many hearts. Living in underground tunnels does not give rise to open societies. Religious dogmas can inflame holy wars by objectifying all one's enemies. Hatred without discipline and rules can perpetuate the cycle without end.

The key implication of the distinction between the "American people" and the "American aggressors" was that the Vietnamese were ultimately pursuing a political-diplomatic strategy, not an exclusively military one. They saw the war ending when the American troops and public opinion decided it was no longer in their interest and all other options were closed. That strategy required a negotiated peace accord to determine whether or not a "final uprising" would occur, a process lasting through the seven long years of the Paris peace talks.

This is not to say that the Vietnamese who were loyal to Hanoi and the National Liberation Front were saintly people who transcended the everyday furies of war. But there was and still is something unusual about the Vietnamese "other side," then and now. Thousands of American tourists today, including countless American veterans who traded fire with National Liberation Front guerrillas, typically express surprise at how friendly and welcoming their former enemies are, who eagerly seek to forgive, reconcile, and engage in storytelling around tables of tea and cookies with Americans they once fought bitterly. The Vietnamese seem to feel equally surprised at American friendliness. It is an ongoing mystery.

There is no "fog of war." There are only festering memories of loss, suffering, trauma, and unnecessary consequences. To take an example from our own history, the American patriots of the Revolutionary War demonized, tarred and feathered, and deported the fleeing Tories to Canada or England, where they settled and reestablished their Orange Lodges, still entertaining dreams of a British reconquest through military, diplomatic, and economic means. They gave incentives to American slaves to join the British army in exchange for repatriation to England. Later they intervened on the side of the Confederate army, although politically England had bragging rights as the first Western nation to abolish the slave trade. More than a century passed before the United States and the United Kingdom would establish a new bond as allied leaders of the so-called Free World.

The crushing defeat of South Vietnam came after more than a century of its existence as a victim of French colonialism, war, defeat, betrayal, and enforced partition by our country. The myth was established that the French "civilizing mission" led to a more cultivated and cosmopolitan Hanoi. Forgotten was the effort by many in the centurion class to overthrow the French state.

With the complete collapse of the Saigon government and armed forces in 1975, a nightmare unfolded that shocked the entire U.S. national security class for decades to come. Complete surrender, unlike negotiated political agreements, led to bitter and brutal consequences. What were the victorious Vietnamese to do about their defeated foes? Similar questions arose after the Cuban Revolution when, with backing from Democrats, Republicans, and the CIA, the most hated Batistianos were executed by firing squads, there was a massive exodus to Miami, and the war was exported across the Florida Straits. Only fifty-five years later could the parties sign and implement a recognition-and-reconciliation agreement, one still sharply contested by Cuban exiles and the Republican right wing.

In the case of Vietnam, there was repression, labor, and "reeducation" camps as well as the sudden flight of the "boat people." Many will resort to their own moral compass to judge this outcome. My own view is that it was a predictable result of a war beyond any negotiating. Yes, there was repression and expulsion of millions of South Vietnamese on the U.S. side. Yes, some three hundred thousand of them died on swampy battlefields as "enemies," and never received proper burials or respect for the sacrifices they endured for their cause. Yes, they and their families are due that honor. Even now their sacrifice in the service of the United States is deliberately omitted by the Pentagon's planned commemoration to honor veterans of the war. Congress feared that to recognize them would mean having to pay them the same benefits their American counterparts get. So they, too, are airbrushed from the official history, and thus do they suffer a double betrayal. The fiction that was called the Republic of South Vietnam was erased from history. The option of a "third force" bridging the actual differences of development and culture was soon absorbed in the larger Vietnamese dream of reunification.

In Laos, the CIA's mercenary forces inflicted carnage on the Pathet Lao and innocent people in the countryside. The new state became part of the Indochina Federation led by Vietnam. In a step toward reconciliation, in November 2015, President Obama visited Laos.

Cambodia fell to the insanity of the Khmer Rouge under Chinese direction, until the Vietnamese army lashed back and suppressed them in 1979, when occurred the first of two wars against China.

In the end, 58,000 Americans were dead, 153,000 were wounded seriously enough to require hospitalization, and 75,000 veterans were left severely disabled.

The figures for South Vietnam's armed forces were at least 200,000 dead and 502,000 wounded. The best estimate of civilian Vietnamese war dead is 2 million.

For the Cambodians it was 200,000 dead on the way to the genocide, during which 1.5 million would die. In Laos, 1 million died.

The demeaning and inflated Pentagon "body counts" of "Enemy Killed" were 502,883, and wounded 932,793. Even in the aftermath of defeat, the numbers from the Pentagon's spin machine were beyond the scope of reason.

The economic costs were similarly misrepresented. The Vietnam War threw the American economy off the gold standard as a pillar of the Western world. The war spending enriched a growing industry of military contractors while starving budgets for education, health care, environmental protection, and the War on Poverty.

It's difficult in retrospect for me to declare the war a victory for Vietnam, though its sovereignty, self-determination, and national pride were successfully defended and remained intact. But the cost was enormous and, even at this remove, hard to fathom. What is forever tragic is all the deaths—Vietnamese and American alike—that could have been prevented.

Conclusion

I HAVE SOUGHT IN THIS essay to rescue the Vietnam peace movement from oblivion. Such a historical fate is far different from simply suffering an atrophied memory of the events of fifty years ago. Today Vietnam and the sixties are very much alive in the popular culture, but twisted in our consciousness. Sex, drugs, and rock 'n' roll are staple stereotypes of the time. There also remains a faint legacy that lingers in contemporary calls for "no ground troops" or "no more Vietnams." The tilt of mainstream understanding is toward empathy for American troops: the fifty-eight thousand who lost their lives, the countless veterans who lost their limbs and remain in shabby VA hospitals years after the last screenings of *Coming Home* and *Born on the Fourth of July*.

The controversial question remains: Who lost Vietnam? Who is responsible for all the killings, body counts, and ultimate defeat? A similar politicized question deeply shaped American culture and politics in the fifties: Who lost China?

The blame from the Right and the Establishment is usually fixed on liberals, Democrats, and peace movements—alleged dupes or Communist sympathizers one and all. The blaming is institutionalized within hawkish or neoconservative think tanks from one election cycle to the next. The worst of these torrents of abuse were solidified in McCarthyism, the hearings by Senator Joseph McCarthy into Communists allegedly lodged in Hollywood, labor unions, and especially the liberal wing of the U.S. State Department in the fifties. It was a time of visceral national fear that World War III might break out at any time, including the use of nuclear weapons by alleged enemies in Moscow, Beijing, or Havana.

In this frozen Cold War atmosphere, as I have already noted, subpoenas were drafted against screenwriters, conspiracies were hatched against priests, and intellectuals were fired, imprisoned, or driven into shadows of anonymity. Scapegoating rose to feverish levels as Richard Nixon pictured Jane Fonda as a reincarnation of the Hollywood Ten, and Daniel Ellsberg was seen as another Alger Hiss. J. Edgar Hoover continually fed the false narratives with his manipulations, counterintelligence, and spying against the peace movement and the entire New Left. In a May 1968 Hoover memo, I was listed among those who needed to be "neutralized."

When Johnson ordered a CIA investigation in 1968 into Communist infiltration of the peace movement, the final version was handed only to the president and his advisor Walt W. Rostow. The report refuted any notion that the young revolutionaries were agents of Moscow, Beijing, or Havana. The document itself was not released publicly until 1997, thirty years later and long after the war had ended. Nevertheless the propaganda spewed on.

It was a faith-based assault led in large part by the fierce anti-Communism of the Catholic Church, symbolized by such celebrated missionaries as Tom Dooley, who touched many an idealistic heart in my Catholic schools. True to past templates were the well-financed, CIA-backed networks known as the China Lobby and the Vietnam Lobby (others would follow to subvert Cuba and Nicaragua).

Some of these anti-Communist lobbies were crude while others were intensely ideological. Just to take a single example, in October 1963 I was escorted into a New York meeting with the mysterious CIA-supported Joseph Buttinger, who was the founder of the CIA's American Friends of Vietnam, the leading lobby for the war, founded in 1955. I don't recall ever seeing a more beautiful personal library, with scores upon scores of books about Vietnam in many languages on ascending circular staircases. Obviously I was impressed as a young student exploring Vietnam. Buttinger's anti-Communist credentials included participation in anti-Nazi undergrounds in Europe. Our meeting was promoted by the social democratic (and ideologically anti-Communist) editors of *Dissent* magazine, including Irving Howe and Michael Harrington. Buttinger would become the leading financier of *Dissent* for several years.

But as Buttinger and I talked in our comfortable leather chairs, it became clear to me that an anti-Communist Cold War ideology animated my host's perspective on every level. Taking military and covert action against Vietnam's Communist state was his most important priority. Since Vietnam would tip the Cold War balance toward a Soviet alliance, it had to be stopped in its tracks by a policy known as regime change, underlaid by liberal anti-Communism. Harrington and Howe shared the same view at the time. So did many friends of mine, including former *Michigan Daily* editor Peter Eckstein, who served as a CIA anti-Communist editor of European student publications, and even the young Gloria Steinem, who was agitating to break Communist-funded student movements around the world. All of these intelligent liberal, even socialist, people were in the thrall of Cold War anti-Communism without any realistic sense of how the Vietnam War might be ended.

The 1962 *Port Huron Statement* forthrightly condemned the ideology and system of communism, so what was the anti-Communist complaint? It was partly rooted in sectarian feuds between Stalinists, Trotskyists, social democrats, and liberals in the thirties. But at its base was a disagreement about the nature of the Vietnam War itself. Those of us in the New Left, facing an arbitrary draft of an unknown war, threw ourselves into researching the roots of Vietnam, which became the basis of the massive teach-ins on many campuses. Robert Scheer's 1965 pamphlet *How the United States Got Involved in Vietnam* and my 1966 book with Staughton Lynd, *The Other Side*, were the results of a new generation's consciousness.

While we ourselves were anti-Communist, our studies concluded that Vietnam was really about nationalism and anticolonialism, and far beyond the capacities of white Western troops to contain or suppress. It was true that Vietnam's nationalist revolution was led by a Communist Party, an armed and clandestine one, with front organizations to mobilize different sectors of the country (women, unions, minorities from the Central Highlands, and so forth). It was true that the party was nationwide. It was further true that Ho Chi Minh was its popular leader and would have been elected president. When John Foster Dulles and the United States scuttled the 1954 Geneva Agreement, they were preventing the nationwide election of Ho Chi Minh and making war inevitable. Their only option was supplementing the defeated French with weapons and advisors. But the rotating Saigon regimes taking up the new White Man's Burden, starting with the Catholic dictator Ngo Dinh Diem, were hapless and corrupt. Diem was cultivated in Catholic seminaries by the U.S. Vietnam Lobby before he unleashed military and police forces against the Communists, nationalists, and saffron-robed bonzes representing the country's Buddhist majority. Then, bizarrely, the JFK administration allowed rival Saigon generals to assassinate Diem in his own car, ending any possibility of reported peace feelers between Diem and Hanoi or the southern insurgency then developing.

In the Cold War perspective, places like South Vietnam were defined as mere "dominoes" doomed to fall under insidious Communist aggression. But would a Communist regime in Hanoi have been more horrifying than the bloodbath that killed and displaced several million Vietnamese? Weren't there other options, such as Tito's Communist-led Yugoslavia, which was seeking autonomy within the Soviet bloc? Seeking their own Cold War triumph over the United States, both the Soviet bloc and China sent massive aid to Vietnam for more than a decade, neutralizing every step in escalation by Washington. Soon enough one American general said we were fighting their birthrate. The term *quagmire* finally entered our political vocabulary in the mid- to late sixties, as the only course of action seemed to be permanent escalation.

Losing is the hardest experience. But a commitment to be "better dead than red" led tens of thousands of American soldiers to their graves in honor of a lost cause.

In this sea of blood the peace movement was born. The moral tragedies of the war, televised for all to see, commingled with the relentless military draft to force us into action. What began with the 1965 teach-ins evolved within a year to draft evasion and draft resistance. Petitioning our government was supplemented by direct action. National and regional peace demonstrations grew to be the largest in our nation's history. We expanded the ranks of protestors on campuses from twenty-five thousand to millions. We spread next to the U.S. bases, barracks, ships at sea, and military recruitment centers. The resistance triggered the inevitable entry of hundreds of elected officials to our cause, from Ron Dellums and Bella Abzug to presidential candidates. As the mainstream opportunities expanded, most of the peace movement moderated, becoming "clean for Gene" or basing its resistance in faith communities. The polls showed a majority of Americans believing the Vietnam War was our Great Mistake.

The new McCarthyism emboldened our ranks. Like the McCarthyism of old, its mad path of escalation far exceeded the norms and laws of our country. At Kent State the reaction turned lethal when National Guardsmen, feeding on false propaganda, turned on a sunny hillside and shot eighteen student

demonstrators, killing four on the campus grounds. Why? The
students were not to blame for their own death, as several historians would imply. It was because the Nixon administration,
including the hotheaded John Dean, whipped up Republicans against "brownshirts" who needed to be eliminated. The
man who used that term was Governor James Rhodes, then in
a close primary race against the peace-leaning Robert Taft for
a Senate seat. Two weeks later, at Mississippi State, police shot
and killed two young black men in their dormitories. Those
murdered would be long remembered as innocent martyrs.
Today they are memorialized in a beautiful education center
on the campus and in annual conferences and peace vigils
where their bodies lay.

Few in American politics want to memorialize the patriotism, strength, and impact of the peace movement during
those ten terrible years. Even many liberals flinch from re-
membering, distancing themselves from the peace movement because the association might affect their careers and
reputations. Barack Obama, early in his tenure as president,
was an example of this. He would dismiss the sixties as a time
of irrational tempests in the generation preceding his own. He
would honor movement heroes who came before, like Harriet
Tubman, with her trusted long gun, during the Underground
Railroad, or the slaves who rose up against their wicked mas-
ters. He would not, however, recognize the Vietnam peace
movement.

But in his last months in office, Obama undertook a shift
on Vietnam, and perhaps even on the peace movement. His
politics had taken form under the influence of Cold War anti-

Communism, and he had an absolute belief that he could never be seen as soft on Communism. Pulling the other way, in his own life, he was strongly influenced by anticolonialism and civil rights. He may have shifted again in his legacy years. Perhaps he realized that on Vietnam, he had been more cautious than audacious.

During his 2016 official visit to Vietnam, Obama stepped into friendly street crowds to become the first president to gaze on the curious faces of the first people who ever had defeated the United States government at war and reconciled in peace. On every historic level, the shift underway was more profound than words could fully express. Obama chose at one moment to step free of the official handlers, and asked to visit the small hatch-roofed house on stilts where Ho Chi Minh sat feeding his fish during retreats, interviews, and rests. Footage from the event shows Obama being tutored about how the Vietnamese feed the fish by hand from a bucket. He practiced once, gained his host's positive approval, and learned to throw some fish in another bucket. The people watched and nodded, including children Obama's children's age.

What he said next was in the language of the early Vietnam peace movement itself, especially speeches by historians like Staughton Lynd and Howard Zinn. In an address to the people of Vietnam, President Obama spoke to what he called our "shared values." It was Obama's clearest repudiation of Cold War thinking thus far.

"During the Second World War, Americans came here to support your struggle against occupation. When American pilots were shot down, the Vietnamese people helped

rescue them. And on the day that Vietnam declared its independence, crowds took to the streets of this city, and Ho
Chi Minh evoked the American Declaration of Independence. He said, 'All people are created equal. The Creator has
endowed them with inalienable rights. Among these rights
are the right to life, the right to liberty, and the right to the
pursuit of happiness.'"

At a state luncheon with President Quang of Vietnam,
Obama offered a toast, saying, "We thank Secretary [John]
Kerry and all our veterans here today, both Vietnamese and
American, who had the courage not only to fight, but, more
importantly, had the courage to make peace."

Later that year, in September 2016, in Laos, Obama
matched words with deeds. He was the first U.S. president
to visit Laos, and the first to say this: "Over nine years, from
1964 to 1973, the United States dropped more than two million tons of bombs here in Laos—more than we dropped on
Germany and Japan combined during all of World War II.
Given our history here, I believe that the United States has a
moral obligation to help Laos heal." Then he announced that
the United States was doubling its annual funding to $90 million over the next three years to vastly speed up the removal
of unexploded U.S. bombs.

His 2016 steps and statements have raised expectations for
Obama's coming years as a former-president global peacemaker. As Jimmy Carter and Bill Clinton have shown, a
former president can accomplish wonders, and there is plenty
to do: assisting Agent Orange victims, both Vietnamese and
U.S. veterans and their affected children; cleaning up cluster

bombs, land mines, and other deadly ordnances; aiding mine victims and providing reconstruction assistance; mitigating lethal environmental damage, and so on.

The task of writing and telling our history, however, is not one we can entrust to anyone else. It is up to us, those who pledged to one another our lives, our fortunes, and our sacred honor to stop the war. Many have already written fine memoirs and books, but there is much more to be told. Mistakes were made, serious mistakes, but our America is a better place because we stood up against all odds.

Further Reading

Albert, Judith Clavir, and Stewart Edward Albert, eds. *The Sixties Papers: Documents of a Rebellious Decade.* New York: Praeger, 1984.

Appy, Christian G. *American Reckoning: The Vietnam War and Our National Identity.* New York: Viking, 2015.

Baez, Joan. *And a Voice to Sing With: A Memoir.* New York: Summit Books, 1987.

Baskir, Lawrence M., and William A. Strauss. *Chance and Circumstance: The Draft, the War and the Vietnam Generation.* New York: Vintage Books, 1978.

Beattie, Keith. *The Scar That Binds: American Culture and the Vietnam War.* New York: New York University Press, 2000.

Berman, Larry. *No Peace, No Honor: Nixon, Kissinger, and Betrayal in Vietnam.* New York: Free Press, 2001.

———. *Planning a Tragedy: The Americanization of the War in Vietnam.* New York: Norton, 1982.

Bernstein, Carl, and Bob Woodward. *All the President's Men.* New York: Warner Books, 1976.

Bills, Scott. *Kent State / May 4: Echoes Through a Decade.* Kent, Ohio: Kent State University Press, 1988.

Bradley, Doug, and Craig Werner. *We Gotta Get out of This Place: The Soundtrack of the Vietnam War.* Amherst: University of Massachusetts Press, 2015.

Braestrup, Peter. *Big Story: How the American Press and Television Reported and Interpreted the Crisis of Tet 1968 in Vietnam and Washington.* Garden City, NY: Anchor/Doubleday, 1978.

Cannon, Lou. *Governor Reagan: His Rise to Power.* New York: PublicAffairs, 2003.

Caputo, Philip. *A Rumor of War.* New York: Ballantine Books, 1984.

———. *13 Seconds: A Look Back at the Kent State Shootings.* New York: Penguin, 2005.

Chomsky, Noam. *At War with Asia.* New York: Vintage Books, 1970.

Churchill, Ward, and Jim Vander Wall. *The COINTELPRO Papers: Documents from the FBI's Secret Wars Against Domestic Dissent.* Boston: South End, 1990.

Clavir, Judy, and John Spitzer, eds. *The Conspiracy Trial.* Indianapolis: Bobbs-Merrill, 1970.

Cobb, Charles. *On the Road to Freedom.* Chapel Hill, NC: Algonquin, 2008.

Coffin, William Sloan, Jr. *Once to Every Man: A Memoir.* New York: Atheneum, 1977.

Cohen, Robert. *Freedom's Orator: Mario Savio and the Radical Legacy of the 1960s.* New York: Oxford University Press, 2009.

Cooper, Chester L. *The Lost Crusade: America in Vietnam.* New York: Dodd, Mead, 1970.

Cortright, David. *Soldiers in Revolt: The American Military Today.* Garden City, NY: Anchor/Doubleday, 1975.

Dancis, Bruce. *Resister.* Ithaca, NY: Cornell University Press, 2014.

Davis, Laura, and Carol Barbatto. *Democratic Narratives.* Kansas City: Kansas State University Press, 2012.

Dean, John. *Blind Ambition: The White House Years.* New York: Pocket Books, 1977.

DeBenedetti, Charles, with Charles Chatfield. *An American Ordeal: The Antiwar Movement of the Vietnam Era.* Syracuse, NY: Syracuse University Press, 1990.

Donner, Frank J. *The Age of Surveillance: The Aims and Methods of*

America's Political Intelligence System. New York: Vintage
Books, 1981.
DuBois, W. E. B. *Black Reconstruction.* New York: Harcourt, Brace,
1935.
Duffet, John, ed. *Against the Crime of Silence: Proceedings of the
Russell International War Crimes Tribunal.* Flanders, NJ:
O'Hare Books, 1968.
Eckstein, Arthur. *Bad Moon Rising: How the Weather Underground
Beat the FBI and Lost the Revolution.* New Haven, CT: Yale
University Press, 2016.
Egerton, Douglas R. *The Wars of Reconstruction: The Brief, Violent
History of America's Most Progressive Era.* New York: Blooms-
bury, 2014.
Ehrlichman, John. *Witness to Power: The Nixon Years.* New York:
Simon & Schuster, 1982.
Ellsberg, Daniel. *Papers on the War.* New York: Simon & Schuster,
1972.
———. *Secrets: A Memoir of Vietnam and the Pentagon Papers.* New
York: Viking, 2002.
Emerson, Gloria. *Winners & Losers: Battles, Retreats, Gains, Losses
and Ruins from a Long War.* New York: Random House, 1977.
FitzGerald, Frances. *America Revised: History Schoolbooks in the
Twentieth Century.* Boston: Little, Brown, 1979.
Flacks, Richard. *Making History: The American Left and the Ameri-
can Mind.* New York: Columbia University Press, 1988.
Flacks, Richard, and Nelson Lichtenstein, eds. *The Port Huron State-
ment: Sources and Legacies of the New Left's Founding Mani-
festo.* Philadelphia: University of Pennsylvania Press, 2015.
Foner, Eric. *Freedom's Lawmakers: A Directory of Black Officehold-
ers During Reconstruction.* New York: Oxford University Press,
1993.
———. *Reconstruction: America's Unfinished Revolution, 1863–1877.*
New York: Harper & Row, 1988.
Foner, Philip. *American Labor and the Indochina War.* New York:
International, 1971.
Garrow, David J. *Bearing the Cross: Martin Luther King, Jr., and*

the Southern Christian Leadership Conference. New York: Morrow, 1986.

Gentry, Curt. J. *Edgar Hoover: The Man and the Secrets*. New York: Norton, 1991.

Gilmore, Glenda Elizabeth. *Defying Dixie: The Radical Roots of Civil Rights, 1919–1950*. New York: Norton, 2008.

Gitlin, Todd. *The Sixties: Years of Hope, Days of Rage*. New York: Bantam Books, 1987.

———. *The Whole World Is Watching: Mass Media in the Making and Unmaking of the New Left*. Berkeley: University of California Press, 1980.

Goldstein, Gordon M. *Lessons in Disaster: McGeorge Bundy and the Path to War in Vietnam*. New York: Times Books / Henry Holt, 2008.

Goodale, James. C. *Fighting for the Press: The Inside Story of the Pentagon Papers and Other Battles*. New York: CUNY Journalism, 2013.

Goodman, Mitchell, ed. *The Movement Toward a New America: The Beginnings of a Long Revolution*. New York: Knopf, 1970.

Grace, Thomas M. *Kent State: Death and Dissent in the Long Sixties*. Amherst: University of Massachusetts Press, 2016.

Greiner, Bernd. *War Without Fronts: The USA in Vietnam*. New Haven, CT: Yale University Press, 2009.

Hagopian, Patrick. *The Vietnam War in American Memory: Veterans, Memorials, and the Politics of Healing*. Amherst: University of Massachusetts Press, 2011.

Halberstam, David. *The Best and the Brightest*. New York: Random House, 1972.

Hall, Mitchell K. *Because of Their Faith: CALCAV and Religious Opposition to the Vietnam War*. New York: Columbia University Press, 1990.

Halstead, Fred. *Out Now! A Participant's Account of the American Movement Against the Vietnam War*. New York: Mondad, 1978.

Harris, David. *Dreams Die Hard*. New York: St. Martin's / Marek, 1982.

————. *I Shoulda Been Home Yesterday*. New York: Delacorte, 1976.

————. *Our War: What We Did in Vietnam and What It Did To Us*. New York: Times Books / Random House, 1996.

Harris, Louis. *The Anguish of Change*. New York: Norton, 1973.

Hayden, Tom. *The Long Sixties: From 1960 to Barack Obama*. Boulder, CO: Paradigm, 2009.

————. *Rebellion in Newark: Official Violence and Ghetto Response*. New York: Vintage, 1967.

————. *Reunion: A Memoir*. New York: Random House, 1988.

Heath, Louis G., ed. *Mutiny Does Not Happen Lightly: The Literature of the American Resistance to the Vietnam War*. Metuchen, NJ: Scarecrow, 1976.

Heinl, Col. Robert D., Jr. "The Collapse of the Armed Forces." *Armed Forces Journal*, June 7, 1971. American Friends Service Committee reprint.

Hendrickson, Paul. *The Living and the Dead: Robert McNamara and Five Lives of a Lost War*. New York: Knopf, 1996.

Herring, George C. *America's Longest War: The United States and Vietnam, 1950–1975*. Philadelphia: Temple University Press, 1986.

Hersh, Seymour M. *My Lai 4: A Report on the Massacre and Its Aftermath*. New York: Random House, 1970.

————. *The Price of Power: Kissinger in the Nixon White House*. New York: Summit Books, 1983.

Hoffman, Paul. *Moratorium: An American Protest*. New York: Tower, 1970.

Isaacson, Walter, and Evan Thomas. *The Wise Men: Six Men and the World They Made*. New York: Simon & Schuster, 1986.

Jeffreys-Jones, Rhodri. *Peace Now! American Society and the Ending of the Vietnam War*. New Haven, CT: Yale University Press, 1999.

Joseph, Paul. *Cracks in the Empire: State Politics in the Vietnam War*. Boston: South End, 1981.

Kaiser, David. *American Tragedy: Kennedy, Johnson, and the Origins of the Vietnam War*. Cambridge, MA: Belknap Press, Harvard University Press, 2000.

Kaplan, Fred. *The Insurgents: David Petraeus and the Plot to Change the American Way of War.* New York: Simon & Schuster, 2013.

Karnow, Stanley. *Vietnam: A History.* New York: Penguin Books, 1991.

Kerry, John, and Vietnam Veterans Against the War. *The New Soldier.* New York: Macmillan, 1971.

Kieran, David. *Forever Vietnam: How a Divisive War Changed American Public Memory.* Amherst: University of Massachusetts Press, 2014.

Kiernan, Ben. *The Pol Pot Regime: Race, Power, and Genocide in Cambodia under the Khmer Rhouge, 1975–79.* New Haven, CT: Yale University Press, 1996.

King, Martin Luther, Jr. "Declaration of Independence from the War in Vietnam." *Ramparts*, May 1967.

Kissinger, Henry. *Years of Upheaval.* Boston: Little, Brown, 1982.

———. *White House Years.* Boston: Little, Brown, 1979.

Kolko, Gabriel. *Anatomy of a War: Vietnam, the United States and the Modern Historical Experience.* New York: Pantheon, 1985.

Kovic, Ron. *Born on the Fourth of July.* New York: McGraw-Hill, 1976.

Kutler, Stanley I. *The Wars of Watergate: The Last Crisis of Richard Nixon.* New York: Knopf, 1990.

Lake, W. Anthony, ed. *The Vietnam Legacy.* New York: New York University Press, 1976.

Lang, Serge. *The Scheer Campaign.* New York: W. A. Benjamin, 1967.

Languuth, A. J. *Our Vietnam: The War, 1954–1975.* New York: Simon & Schuster, 2000.

Larner, Jeremy. *Nobody Knows: Reflections on the McCarthy Campaign of 1968.* New York: Macmillan, 1970.

Larteguy, Jean. *The Centurions: A Novel.* New York: Penguin, 2015.

Lee, Martin, and Bruce Shlain. *Acid Dreams: The Complete Social History of LSD; The CIA, the Sixties, and Beyond.* New York: Grove, 1993.

Lembcke, Jerry. *The Spitting Image: Myth, Memory, and the Legacy of Vietnam.* New York: New York University Press, 1998.

Lerner, Michael P. "May Day: Anatomy of the Movement." *Ramparts*, July 1971.

Lewes, James. *Protest and Survive: Underground GI Newspapers During the Vietnam War.* Santa Barbara, CA: Praeger, 2003.

Lifton, Robert Jay. *Home from the War: Learning from Vietnam Veterans.* New York: Simon & Schuster, 1973.

Lipset, Seymour Martin, and Sheldon Wolin. *The Berkeley Student Revolt.* New York: Anchor/Doubleday, 1965.

Logevall, Fredrik. *Choosing War: The Lost Chance for Peace and the Escalation of War in Vietnam.* Berkeley: University of California Press, 1999.

———. *Embers of War: The Fall of an Empire and the Making of America's Vietnam.* New York: Random House, 2012.

Lukas, J. Anthony. *Nightmare: The Underside of the Nixon Years.* New York: Viking, 1976.

Lynd, Alice, ed. *We Won't Go: Personal Accounts of War Objectors.* Boston: Beacon, 1968.

Lynd, Staughton, and Michael Ferber. *The Resistance.* Boston: Beacon, 1970.

Lynd, Staughton, and Thomas Hayden. *The Other Side.* New York: New American Library, 1966.

Lytle, Mark Hamilton. *America's Uncivil Wars: The Sixties Era from Elvis to the Fall of Richard Nixon.* New York: Oxford University Press, 2006.

Mailer, Norman. *The Armies of the Night.* New York: New American Library, 1968.

Maraniss, David. *They Marched into Sunlight: War and Peace, Vietnam and America, October 1967.* New York: Simon & Schuster, 2003.

Mariscal, Jorge. *Aztlan and Viet Nam: Chicano and Chicana Experiences of the War.* Berkeley: University of California Press, 1999.

Martini, Edwin A. *Invisible Enemies: The American War on Vietnam, 1975–2000.* Amherst: University of Massachusetts Press, 2007.

McAdam, Doug. *Freedom Summer.* New York: Oxford University Press, 1988.

McCarthy, Mary. *Vietnam.* New York: Harcourt, Brace & World, 1967.

McNamara, Robert S., with Brian Van De Mark. *In Retrospect: The*

Tragedy and Lessons of Vietnam. New York: Times Books / Random House, 1995.

Medsger, Betty. *The Burglary: The Discovery of J. Edgar Hoover's Secret FBI.* New York: Knopf, 2014.

Menashe, Louis, and Ronald Radosh, eds. *Teach-ins: U.S.A.* New York: Praeger, 1967.

Michel, Marshall, III. *The Eleven Days of Christmas.* San Francisco: Encounter Books, 2002.

Michener, James. *Kent State.* New York: Fawcett, 1971.

Miller, James. *"Democracy Is in the Streets": From Port Huron to the Siege of Chicago.* New York: Simon & Schuster, 1987.

Moise, Edwin E. *Tonkin Gulf and the Escalation of the Vietnam War.* Chapel Hill: University of North Carolina Press, 1996.

Morrison, Joan, and Robert K. Morrison, eds. *From Camelot to Kent State: The Sixties Experience in the Words of Those Who Lived It.* New York: Times Books, 1987.

Neale, Jonathan. *A People's History of the Vietnam War.* New York: New Press, 2003.

Nguyen, Viet Thanh. *Nothing Ever Dies: Vietnam and the Memory of War.* Cambridge, MA: Harvard University Press, 2016.

Nicosia, Gerald. *Home to War: A History of the Vietnam Veterans' Movement.* New York: Crown, 2001.

Ninh, Bao. *The Sorrow of War: A Novel of North Vietnam.* New York: Pantheon, 1995.

Oudes, Bruce, ed. *From: The President; Richard Nixon's Secret Files.* New York: Harper & Row, 1989.

Paget, Karen. *Patriotic Betrayal: The Inside Story of the CIA's Secret Campaign to Enroll American Students in the Crusade Against Communism.* New Haven, CT: Yale University Press, 2015.

Patterson, James. *The Eve of Destruction.* New York: Basic Books, 2012.

Payne, Charles. *I've Got the Light of Freedom: The Organizing Tradition and the Mississippi Freedom Struggle.* Berkeley: University of California Press, 1995.

The Pentagon Papers. Senator Gravel ed. 5 vols. Boston: Beacon, 1971.

The Pentagon Papers as Published by the "New York Times." New York: Bantam Books, 1971.

Perlstein, Rick. *Nixonland: The Rise of a President and the Fracturing of America.* New York: Scribner, 2008.

Perry, Lewis. *Civil Disobedience: An American Tradition.* New Haven, CT: Yale University Press, 2013.

Ponchaud, Francois. *Cambodia: Year Zero.* New York: Holt, Rinehart, Winston, 1978.

Powers, Thomas. *Vietnam: The War at Home.* New York: Grossman, 1973.

Rosales, Arturo. *Chicano! The History of the Mexican American Civil Rights Movement.* Houston: Arte Publico, 1997.

Rosenberg, Milton U. J., Sidney Verba, and Philip E. Converse. *Vietnam and the Silent Majority: The Dove's Guide.* New York: Harper & Row, 1970.

Rudenstine, David. *The Day the Presses Stopped: A History of the Pentagon Papers Case.* Berkeley: University of California Press, 1996.

Sale, Kirkpatrick. *SDS.* New York: Random House, 1973.

Salisbury, Harrison E., ed. *Vietnam Reconsidered: Lessons from a War.* New York: Harper & Row, 1984.

Scheer, Robert. *How the United States Got Involved in Vietnam.* Santa Barbara, CA: Center for the Study of Democratic Institutions, 1965.

Schell, Jonathan. *The Time of Illusion.* New York: Vintage Books, 1976.

Shapley, Deborah. *Promise and Power: The Life and Times of Robert McNamara.* Boston: Little, Brown, 1993.

Shawcross, William. *Sideshow: Kissinger, Nixon and the Destruction of Cambodia.* New York: Simon & Schuster, 1979.

Sheehan, Neil. *A Bright Shining Lie: John Paul Vann and America in Vietnam.* New York: Random House, 1988.

Skolnick, Jerome. *The Politics of Protest.* New York: Ballantine Books, 1969.

Smith, Paul Chatt, and Robert Allen Warrior. *Like a Hurricane: The Indian Movement from Alcatraz to Wounded Knee.* New York: New Press, 1996.

Sontag, Susan. *Trip to Hanoi.* New York: Farrar, Straus & Giroux, 1968.

Terzani, Tiziano. *Giai Phong! The Fall and Liberation of Saigon*. New York: St. Martin's, 1976.

Tin, Bui. *From Enemy to Friend: A North Vietnamese Perspective on the War*. Annapolis, MD: Naval Institute Press, 2002.

Turse, Nick. *Kill Anything That Moves: The Real American War in Vietnam*. New York: Metropolitan Books, 2013.

Vietnam Day Committee. *We Accuse*. Berkeley: Diablo, 1965.

The Vietnam Hearings. New York: Vintage Books, 1966.

Walker, Daniel. *Rights in Conflict: The Violent Confrontation of Demonstrators and Police in the Parks and Streets of Chicago During the Week of the Democratic National Convention of 1968*. New York: Bantam Books, 1968.

Weiner, Tim. *Legacy of Ashes: A History of the CIA*. New York: Doubleday, 2007.

———. *One Man Against the World: The Tragedy of Richard Nixon*. New York: Henry Holt, 2015.

Wells, Tom. *The War Within: America's Battle over Vietnam*. Berkeley: University of California Press, 1994.

Werner, Jayne, and Luu Doanh Huynh. *The Vietnam War: Vietnamese and American Perspectives*. London: Routledge, 2015.

Wolin, Richard. *Wind from the East: French Intellectuals, the Cultural Revolution, and the Legacy of the 1960s*. Princeton, NJ: Princeton University Press, 2010.

Woodward, Bob. *Obama's Wars*. New York: Simon & Schuster, 2010.

Woodward Bob, and Carl Bernstein. *The Final Days*. New York: Avon Books, 1977.

Zaroulis, Nancy, and Gerald Sullivan. *Who Spoke Up? American Protest Against the War in Vietnam, 1963–1975*. Garden City, NY: Doubleday, 1984.

Zimmerman, Bill. *Troublemaker: A Memoir from the Front Lines of the Sixties*. New York: Doubleday, 2011.

Zinn, Howard. *The Bomb*. San Francisco: City Lights, 2010.

Acknowledgments

MY DEEPEST THANKS TO Steve Wasserman, editor at large at Yale University Press and now publisher of Heyday Books in Berkeley, California. He urged me to write this book and had the confidence that its publication would help rescue the Vietnam peace movement from social amnesia and official oblivion. I've known Steve since 1969, and he and I always have been close in thinking. This book would never have been finished without his guidance, deep knowledge, editorial skills, and care.

I extend my gratitude to Paul Ryder, a brilliant researcher, and his wife, Susan Wind Early, a superb graphic and design artist. My friendship with both goes back to the time of the Indochina Peace Campaign when a handful of people devoted several years to tasks such as humanizing the culture of the Vietnamese, researching and writing about the Pentagon Papers, and getting arrested by the Thieu dictatorship in dangerous wartime Saigon. Their skills have only deepened with the decades, and they should be included on any short list of serious Vietnam experts.

My appreciation also goes to Emma Taylor, a child of the sixties generation, for her attention, focus, and good cheer while struggling through my no-mistakes approach to research and editing. Emma learned an enormous amount about the Vietnam experience of her parents' generation, and has become an invaluable, extremely grounded assistant in her own right.

This book would not have been possible without the loving support of my wife, Barbara, and our brilliant, budding sixteen-year-old son, Liam. Somehow Barbara finished an incandescent memoir of her own, *The Hope in Leaving*, published by Seven Stories Press, during this tumultuous year, and has proven to be a better, more poetic author than I shall ever be. Liam is turning into a mature young man, getting good grades and looking forward to our college tour next year.

I want to thank my former wife, Jane Fonda, and our son, Troy Garity, for the years we all struggled through the crisis of Vietnam. Jane took completely unjustified blows from the Republican Right, which needed a scapegoat. I will say this about the devoted Republican Right: they never quit and they never will. As to Troy, he and his sister, Vanessa, he now in Los Angeles and she in Vermont, grew into loving and gifted adults I could not be more proud of. I love my whole family.

Finally, my thanks go to my friends and colleagues who labored tirelessly to organize the massive memorial gathering of the veterans of the Vietnam peace movement on May 1–2,

2015, in Washington, DC, the first reunion of so many old friends who scattered on their own paths after the traumatic war ended. They include many Vietnam veterans who had the courage to turn against the war in its final years as well as many recognized in the pages of this book. I especially thank David Cortright, Marge Tabankin, Heather and Paul Booth, Ira Arlook, Terry Provance, John McAuliff, Alan Charney, and Bill Goodfellow—as well as such heroes as David Harris, Staughton Lynd, Ron Dellums, Barbara Lee, and Pat Schroeder.

We will forever miss and remember our friend Julian Bond, who gave the keynote address at that gathering before passing away just three weeks later.

We are all passing away with the years, whether we are war veterans or peace veterans. Millions of Indochinese peoples are gone already, victims of the cruel and unnecessary policies of American decision makers. Nothing is worse than an unwinnable war except innocent lives sacrificed in vain.

Learning the true lessons of the war is the only possible path to pure forgiveness. My prayer is that such reconciliation takes place in this generation.